A Love Story
Good Grief

Capt R A Jaycox

iUniverse, Inc.
New York   Bloomington

A Love Story   Good Grief

iUniverse books may be ordered through booksellers or by contacting:

iUniverse
1663 Liberty Drive
Bloomington, IN 47403
www.iuniverse.com
1-800-Authors (1-800-288-4677)

ISBN: 978-1-4502-4441-1 (pbk)
ISBN: 978-1-4502-4442-8 (ebk)

Printed in the United States of America

iUniverse rev. date: 8/3/2010

ABOUT THE AUTHORS

Captain Robert A. Jaycox is the author of a memoir, *The Boatswain's Pipe,* a story of his Navy days and years on the water, Lake Erie. He is eighty-three years old, and still runs a charter fishing business on the Great Lakes, called Majestic Charters. He is the father of two children – a son, Bob, Jr. and a daughter, Carol, both of whom are grown and married. Virginia and he have four grandchildren and five great grandchildren. He loves to write and enjoys people. He hopes that people can relate to this book, who, although they believe, they still have questions when they experience a loss so close.

Co-author and editor is Connie Trelka and Captain Jaycox's niece, and she edited Captain Jaycox's first book. She has also written two books regarding World War II, the first about the European Theater, and the second about the Pacific Theater. She is a retired English and History high school teacher with 31 years of service with the Washington School District where she performed many roles besides teaching and administrating. She graduated Phi Beta Kappa and Magna Cum Laude in 1976 from Washington and Jefferson College and received her Master's Degree Educational Psychology in 1984 from the same institution and her Secondary Principal's Certification from California University in 1988. She and her husband of 43 years have two children, a son, Darin, who is an M.D./Ph.D, and a Forensic Pathologist in Florida, and a daughter, Jessica, who has achieved a B.A. from Otterbein College, and an M.M. from Boston University in Musicology. Jessica has also completed some work toward her Ph.D. Connie lives in Washington, Pennsylvania with her husband, Dennis, who is a retired Washington and Jefferson Biology Professor with 36 years of service. She enjoys her retirement and loves to write, to read, and to complete Sunday New York Times crossword puzzles.

DEDICATION

This book, *Good Grief,* is dedicated to my late wife, Virginia Jaycox, who died on September 15th, 2007. She was a beautiful woman in heart and body. Her warm smile and gentle words made her a loveable, loyal friend to all she met. All references to religious beliefs mentioned in this book are only brought to light as an attempt to raise the questions one might have as he or she processes grief from the catastrophic loss of a loved one. In some cases, I have attempted to play "Devil's Advocate," not literally, I might add, but to clarify some statements of belief. This book makes no claim either way respective to anyone's religious creeds, but simply asks some questions as to the mysteries of death when grief consumes us. Written by Capt. R. A. Jaycox and co-authored by Connie Trelka, we hope to share the ambiguity of the psychology of grief and to point out how we may experience the phenomena of the hereafter.

EDITOR'S NOTE

A little more than two years ago, I volunteered to assist my uncle, Captain Robert Jaycox, to write his memoirs, *The Boatswain's Pipe*. It was a fun and easy job, because all that I had to do was to "spiff" up his grammar and spelling, as well as to put certain incidents in chronological order. The story was educational and fun to write and to read.

That July in 2007, I met with him and my Aunt Dinny to solidify our plans for the book. For years my aunt had been suffering with a food absorption problem which caused her too much discomfort and dramatic weight loss. I believe this very tall, very well-built woman was now wearing the smallest junior sizes, and she appeared to be very gaunt. Aunt Dinny had to have a shunt inserted in her body to deliver nutrition which was to help her to become stronger in order to endure an operation in two months. We were all hopeful that this would be the last operation, and that she would be cured once and for all. She had the best surgeon in the area, yet she was ambivalent about going to the hospital, yet again, for all of the other visits failed to cure her ailment.

The following is a love story and a journal of handling the grief of losing a wife, a mother, and a sister. It includes some answers to the questions that my uncle sought from others regarding where his life-long love, Virginia, is now; if she would remember or recognize my uncle when he passes away and joins her.

It was a difficult story for my uncle to write and for me to edit, because it was too close to both of us for objectivity, yet the reader will understand the depth of his grief and breadth of his love for her. This is an extraordinary effort for an eighty-two year-old-man to articulate. Elizabeth Kubler-Ross's five stages of grief – Denial, Anger, Bargaining, Depression, and Acceptance – are evident throughout this memoir. It was a sixty-two year romance, and his love for Virginia continues to sustain him.

Connie Trelka, M. A.

INTRODUCTION

My wife, Virginia, was still a statuesque blonde at the age of eighty. Her life had not been easy for the past thirty years due to recurring health problems, and the corrective surgeries that seemed to worsen her quality of life, yet she never complained. This lovely woman continuously worried about her children, their children, or other people. She gladly donated to any organization which asked her for financial assistance. Her heart was the most giving, and her smile and good nature drew people to her, which made them love her. We affectionately called her "Dinny." She, I believe, was truly a messenger from God, because of her generosity and compassion for all. She was born into a family of Catholics. Her mother gave birth to fifteen children because of her faith and had instilled the tenets of her religion into each and every one of them. Virginia, although not a church-goer, practiced her mother's faith by treating everyone with love and respect. Our marriage was a beautiful combination of love and compassion for each other. To demonstrate my affection for her, I never forgot to kiss her "good night," and to kiss and to hug her "hello" every morning. She made our lives together a beautiful thing. During our marriage, we were never apart for more than a week or two.

Every weekend, my daughter, Carol, came over to get Virginia to take her to the shopping malls. It became a ritual with them throughout the year. They made their rounds of the malls until they had all of the presents for everyone in the family. Although her health was not good, Dinny never turned down the opportunity to buy for others, or to go out to a restaurant to eat. There were times, however, when she was in so much pain when she returned home, that she sat down in a chair and slept, without moving, for two days.

THE TRAGEDY

Our story begins with the unexpected end of the life of a person who was part of the most beautiful love affair a man has ever experienced, and it lasted for more than sixty years. Think about it! Who, in these modern days, stays with the same person for that length of time? When a person saw me, he or she saw her, and vice versa. I am proud to have known her, to have loved her, to have married her, and to have spent my life with her.

After watching her writhe in pain and waste away from two hundred pounds to one hundred seventeen pounds over a span of years, I finally insisted that we go to a famous major metropolitan hospital to see if the doctors there could properly diagnose her problem. She had experienced a lot of diarrhea which caused not only excruciating pain, but also humiliating embarrassment. When we saw the doctor at the hospital, he evaluated her as having adhesions (scar tissue) that had wrapped around her bowels. The doctor also informed us that we had to build up her metabolism before he could safely operate. Therefore, we took on the job called T.P.N. – Total Protein Nutrition – involving the placing of a feeding tube into an artery, and each night she was connected to a bag of highly refined energy-packed fluid to nourish her body throughout the night. We did that for about four months until her weight grew to be one hundred forty pounds, a point at which her physicians agreed that she was strong enough to undergo the procedure to remove the obstruction in her bowel.

Finally, the day of hope came. On September 13th, we took her over to the health institution. Thirteen was our lucky number, so naturally I was confident that this surgery would finally help her to enjoy life. She was admitted, and she underwent the operation. We were advised that the procedure was a success. After the Recovery Room released her, she was gurneyed to her room to recuperate. My daughter, Carol, and I went over to see her, but she was not aware of us at first because she was hallucinating. I asked the nurse about her condition. I was advised that she may have received too much pain medication. I really began to worry about her when Virginia started making remarks, "I'm not coming home this time." I brushed it off and told her to stop that talk. As Dinny lay there, she eventually became lucid and spoke rationally, because she commented on The Cleveland Indians game that was on her television. Yet, we were still worried, and asked the nurse if we were able to stay and to watch her all night. The nurse assured us that the staff would keep a close eye on her, and that we should go home, which we did, reluctantly.

The next day, the 14th, we let her rest, but at five-thirty on the morning of the 15th, I received a call from a nurse at the hospital, "Your wife has had a bad night; it's bad, but not serious." I asked her what had happened. She advised me, "Your wife has vomited, and inhaled fluid into her lungs. She is okay. We are trying to get the fluid out of her lungs so that she doesn't contract pneumonia." What a nightmare! But, what I didn't know then is how much of a nightmare it was going to be! I asked the nurse if we should come right over, and she informed me to get there before noon. I called my daughter, and she and I drove back to the hospital. We went straight to her room, but it was empty, so I asked the duty nurse about the location of my wife. She informed Carol and me that they had taken her to the Intensive Care Unit. I thought that this was where she should have been after her surgery, not in a regular hospital room. Carol and I went to Intensive Care and saw a group of interns, nurses, and doctors standing around Virginia on a "med bed." When they saw us coming, one girl said, "Oh, here comes her family." As we walked up to her bed, we saw hoses and tubes in her mouth. Air was being pumped into her lungs, and her chest was heaving up and down, as if she were breathing. I looked at her eyes, which were wide open and wrinkled. She looked dead already, but the doctor told me, "She can hear you, if you want to talk to her." I told my daughter, "Don't bother, Carol. She is gone already."

The hospital staff took us into a little room and asked if I wanted to keep her alive on life support. On several occasions, Virginia had told me to avoid continuing her life by using machines. My daughter and I were in total shock. We had walked in on a death, not a fight to remove the fluid from her lungs. The medical personnel claimed that they had revived her three times, and that this was the fourth. I had to tell them to remove the life-lines to the most beautiful, wonderful human being that I had ever known, because of her wishes.

The medicos returned in a few minutes and told us that she was gone.

How my daughter and I ever got home is still a mystery to us. We sobbed until we were exhausted.

After a month passed, I still could not accept the hospital's explanation of her death. I felt that she may have vomited or choked, and there was no one there to assist her to sit up or to take action to help her to recover from choking. If there were someone with her, as they claim, why did she die from vomiting? Good God! People vomit every day in the hospital, and they don't die! There had to be more to the story than was being told to me. Because I was so upset with Virginia's death, and lack of hospital care for her after the surgery, I hired a lawyer, who later sent me a letter detailing that it would cost too much money to fight the hospital and that it was too big and too strong to sue it.

So here I sit, trying to make sense of it all! My beautiful wife is gone. I pray for her every night, hoping that some sign of contact with her will emerge. I have included a poem, which reflects my sense of what Dinny must have felt at her moment of death. It is called, "Safely Home." No one knows who wrote it, but it has given millions of people solace in times of grief. Later in this book, I shall describe the many ways that she has made her presence and her feelings known to me from heaven.

Since I have described the end of the life of the woman I have loved and will continue to love, I shall try to relate the beginning of life for her.

SAFELY HOME

I am home in Heaven, dear ones;
Oh, so happy and so bright;
There is perfect joy and beauty
In this everlasting light.

All the pain and grief is over,
Every restless tossing is passed;
I am now at peace forever,
Safely home in Heaven at last.

Did you wonder I so calmly
Trod the valley of the Shade?
Oh! But Jesus' love illumined
Every dark and fearful glade.

And he came Himself to meet me
In that way so hard to tread;
And with Jesus' arm to lean on,
Could I have one doubt or dread?

Then you must not grieve so sorely,
For I love you dearly still:
Try to look beyond earth's shadows,
Pray to trust our Father's Will.

There is work still waiting for you,
So you must not idly stand;
Do it now, while life remaineth
You shall rest in Jesus' land.

When that work is all completed,
He will gently call you Home;
Oh the rapture of that meeting,
Oh, the joy to see you come!

Author Unknown

My Beloved, My Buddy, My Pal

VIRGINIA'S STORY

Virginia Traxler Jaycox was born on April, 27, 1927, one of nine living children; there would have been thirteen Traxler children, had they all lived – two sets of twins died at birth. Dinny's mother, Mary Hoffman, came to the "States" from Berlin, Germany, in 1919, just after World War I ended. She met and married William Traxler, who was an American citizen. Both were strict Catholics, and they believed in a large family. Virginia was the second youngest of the Traxler brood, growing up during the Great Depression. She actually shared a bed with her older sister, Rita, and her brother, Bill. Her siblings included brothers – Nick, Paul, Bill – and sisters – Pauline, Lucille, Evangeline, Rita, and Gertrude.

Like many families during the Depression, The Traxlers struggled to make ends meet. Although Virginia's father had a good job as a contractor, business was slow due to the economy. The Traxler children were guided by their frail and dour mother, who worked and scrubbed to help her family to survive the rigors of that period in history when so many perished. Dinny remembered her mother as a strict and unhappy woman who was married to a man who drank heavily and who emotionally and physically abused her.

When World War II broke out in December 1941, Virginia donated her time, as a young woman, as a Red Cross volunteer, making bandages for injured service men. While she was too young to join the service, she felt that she needed to help in the war effort in any way possible, as did many other Americans at that time. Two of Dinny's brothers volunteered for war service – one went into the Army; the other joined the Marine Corps.

Dinny loved her mother deeply, and tried to help her with the many chores that needed to be done with a family so large. Late during the War, in

1945, Mary Hoffman Traxler, Virginia's mother, died in her sleep – a complete shock to her entire family. The family watched in horror as the ambulance attendants carried their mother's body out of the door. Because there was no transportation for Dinny to use, she walked four miles to the cemetery to cry on her mother's grave site.

After Mary's death, only Virginia, her sisters and father shared the house, often taking turns looking for their father's car, after nights of binge drinking. Her father, Bill, had a good heart when he was sober, but he drank away his construction business, and eventually the girls had to go to work in order to survive. Dinny and Rita went to work at the American Stove Works, a plant about twenty-five blocks from their home. They walked back and forth to work every day. Rita was the stronger willed of the two, and often looked out for her younger sister. Virginia did not know how to get mad or how to fight, but Rita did. On some occasions, she did physically battle for Dinny. One such event can be found in Rita's chapter.

Virginia and I met in 1947 and were married a couple of months afterward. But I have gotten ahead of myself, because the details of our married life are told in another chapter, "Our Love Story."

VIRGINIA'S PARENTS

William Traxler   *Mary Traxler*

OUR LOVE STORY

Before our love story began, in 1943, I volunteered for naval duty at age 17. Later on in 1944, I met and married a beautiful Irish girl from Salem, Massachusetts. I was shipped out on a destroyer, The U.S.S. Mayrant DD-402, and was sent to the Pacific, and did not see her again until after the war ended in 1945. I mustered out in 1947, returned home, and met my new wife at home in Lorain, Ohio. I found out that she had been married to several other guys at the same time in order to receive our military allotment checks. Needless to say, I suffered from a broken heart.

I tried to ease that pain by racing boats and learning how to fly. During that time I started to date, and one night went out to the local roller skating rink, The Lorain Coliseum, where I spotted a great-looking gal who was spinning around the rink. My cousin, Pauline, was there, so I asked her to introduce me to that beautiful woman, whose name turned out to be Virginia. She was very shy and hard to get to know. As time passed, we became friends, and I began to see her. My divorce was not yet final, but I fell in love with Virginia. Early in the day of our next date, I bought a ring for her to become my wife. While we were driving in my 1939 Ford Coupe, I gave her the ring, and then told her about the situation with my soon-to-be-former wife. When she heard my news, she made me stop the car, which I did immediately. She got out of the car, threw away the ring, and walked home. I was heart-broken again; I loved that woman!

After the divorce was final, I eventually got things patched up again with Dinny, and we were getting along great. In the spring of 1947, I took a job sailing on lake freighters, which took me away from my lovely Virginia. As we sailed past Lorain, I began to feel badly about leaving her. As things generally seem to happen, the Lord figured out how to get us back together again. On the freighter, I got into a fist fight with the captain's "pet" wheelman. I beat him up pretty good, and the skipper put me off the ship. It's ironic how fate takes over things, because later in life, when I became harbormaster, I was giving orders to that captain. At any rate, when I returned home from the ship, I went straight to Dinny's house and asked her to marry me again. She said yes, and we were married on June 27th, 1947, by a Justice of the Peace in Wellington, Ohio.

Our story from then on is one of two people who were in love and worked together as buddies to build a life together. We played; we worked, and loved each other completely.

I continued to complete my cross-country solo flights, and received my pilot's license. Virginia was a great gal with all of the qualities that any man could or would want – she was beautiful, intelligent, faithful, and quite adventurous. One day, I had her meet me in a vacant field out near Vermilion to show her my flying prowess. I got her up in the plane and did a few rolls and loops. Suddenly, she vomited up in the backseat. When I took her back, landed in the field, and flew the plane back to the airport, my instructor asked, "What in the hell happened here?" Later, I took my dad up, and completed a few maneuvers, which scared and maddened him, because he called me, "a crazy bastard," and to get him back to the airport as soon as possible. Dinny was a far better sport than he was; at least she did not swear at me!

I was also somewhat of a boat fanatic. I built a rowboat and began to fish. In 1948, my wife and I were then living in a four-family apartment on West Erie Avenue in Lorain. Our first baby, Bobby, Jr., was on the way, and times were tough. I was working at a gas station on West Erie and Oberlin Avenues, and I graduated to buying a hydroplane boat, which I raced. Virginia supported that purchase, because that is what she did – supported all of my whims, which you will see later!

In the early days around 1950, I worked full time in that gas station and part-time for a moving van company, which used to haul things for businesses and people. One bakery used to have a boxcar full of one hundred pound bags of sugar come in once a month or so. The owners of the bakery gave me the job of unloading the boxcar. One hundred pound bags have no handles, and my hands became hardened to the job, but I recall that Dinny used to soak my hands in Epsom salt and followed it by a lotion massage every time that I had to do the unloading job.

When two people first marry, they think that they are in love, but as the years pass, the couple gains a better insight as to what true love is. Sex is great, but no way can a person build a lasting, loving relationship with another on sex alone. When one's mate hurts, the other feels the hurt. That is when one realizes how powerful an emotion that love is.

In 1960, Virginia and I purchased the fishing tug, The Betty J., and thereafter, she supported me in the purchases of our subsequent fishing tugs. She spent untold hours helping me to string nets for those tugs and she toiled on those tugs as well, removing fish from the nets. Later on, in order to cut our overhead costs, we bought a store, J. and J. Fish, at 14th Street and Broadway in Lorain. Dinny spent hours upon hours filleting the fish that we caught and packing them on ice, either to be sold in the store or to be shipped to other vendors.

Virginia and I always found a way to have fun together. On all of the job ventures that I was involved with, she was always by my side, not because I coerced her, but because she wanted to be there with me. My life has always been around the water, and I almost always had a second job. When I worked for twenty five years as an steam engineer, I fished commercially and ran the fish store. While as a harbormaster, I also ran charters for fishing and tours to McGarvey's in Vermilion for dinner. As a result of trying to make a good living for our family, Dinny raised our children – a boy and a girl. She was like a mother hen to the kids, working hard to make certain that they grew up with values.

Our son, Bobby, was born at 8 pounds in 1948, and survived pneumonia as a nine-year-old. He became interested in baseball and pitched his high school team to a state championship. After high school, he played Class-A ball for Barry Buick in Cleveland until the Vietnam War broke out. My wife and I enjoyed his games when we could go to see them. Bobby decided to join the Army, completing training in Fort Knox, Kentucky, until he was assigned to the First Air Calvary and was sent to Vietnam, where his job was as a radio operator.

I remember that in order to visit him while he was on "R. and R.," (Rest and Recreation) in Hawaii, that we did not have the money to do so, so we took out a second mortgage on our house in order to see our son. While we were on the plane, the stewardess (flight attendant today) accidentally spilled a beverage all over Virginia's top. My wife was mortified because she thought Bobby would see her to be less than beautiful and perfect. The very apologetic young lady took Dinny's blouse and washed and dried it for her. We spent a very wonderful rest of the trip, happy to be with Bobby in paradise.

After that, Bobby was wounded, ending his pitching days. At the end of the war, Bobby came home, received his captain's papers, and was running charters with the boat that Virginia and I bought for him to do so. As fate would have it, just as he was really becoming successful, he lost his license due to complications from his exposure to Agent Orange in Vietnam. He ended up in a Veterans' Administration hospital to have throat surgery – a tracheotomy and a larynjectomy, which resulted in his needing to use an artificial larynx (voice box). He and his daughter bought a farm, and they are now raising chickens, pheasants, and mastiff dogs.

Ten years after Bobby's birth, our daughter, Carol, was born. When I saw her for the first time, I told my wife that the nurses must have mixed up the babies, that this child was not ours. She had coal black hair, dark skin, and looked like she had a big nose. When my wife took the baby into bed with her at the hospital, Dinny squeezed Carol's nose, as if she could have changed it! As time went on, we saw that we had the most beautiful daughter, and she turned out to be a great gal, never giving us a moment of apprehension! After high school, Carol wanted to become an airline stewardess, but flying worried us. Yet, we let her make up her own mind. She began her life's career as a switch-board operator, but over the years, she worked hard, and the company realized her worth, promoting her upward through the ranks, until she became in charge of the Great Lakes Area, as the professional in charge of selling phone services.

Later, when the kids were older Virginia started to share more of an interest in the water, even though she could not swim a stroke. She really seemed to enjoy being on the fish tug with me and the crew. She turned out to be a damn good worker, and she loved it! I recall days when the lake was rough and it was snowing – maybe early in March. She stood at the pulling machine and helped me to bring the fish aboard. Her blond hair was tossed by the wind and blowing snow; she was laughing and joking with all of us. It was quite a sight and very heartwarming, knowing that she loved me so much to work so hard as my helpmate.

Virginia and I were married for thirty-five years by 1981, and we had two children. We were in our fifties, and I was out of a job – no commercial fishing, no harbor-mastering, no money! Yet, Dinny was by my side through the good times and through the tribulations of shutting down our store and our fishing business.

At any rate, my wife and I were determined to go on our annual vacation to Florida, this time to Key Largo, where I started to "wheel and deal" to buy a big, beautiful boat, "The Miss Majestic," to take to Lorain to save the city from obscurity, at least in my mind that was what I hoped to do. I wanted it to get a lot of fishermen on to take charter rides, so that once again, I could be on my beloved lake. When Virginia saw that boat, and understood my intentions, she just stood on the deck and shook her head, saying, "What in the Hell do you want with that monstrosity?" I drove her nuts until she finally relented, after a month of negotiating with the owners, and with the bank; she was ours!

"The Miss Majestic" was a beautiful boat that exacted a beautiful bank loan. We borrowed $185,000 at 19 percent interest. Virginia and I worked so hard during our twelve-plus hour days, taking out fishing charters and running dinner tours to Vermilion. Dinny was there with me to take tickets, to make reservations for the fishing trips and to "chat up" the clients. People came to love her gentle, caring personality.

When the "Haters" came to the fore with their jealous, vindictive methods of cutting dock lines or smearing feces on our gate to the boat, she held her head high and refused to be angry with them. Despite these acts, business was great; payments were huge, but we were never late, nor did we ever miss any payments. During our sixty years together, I do not ever recall her getting mad at anyone but me. Then it was short-lived, because we enjoyed making up!

In 1984, I decided to take "The Miss Majestic" back down to Key Largo for the winter. During our trip, the boat had suffered a damaged propeller, just outside of New York City, and the port engine had to be shut down. With only one engine running, we finally put in at Cape May, not only to have the prop repaired, but also to hunker down to get out of the way of an impending hurricane. While we were laying over at the dock, I went down to the engine room to check out the quality of the repairs that were done. For some reason, Virginia, who was sitting on the deck, suddenly got up and walked through the cabin into the after part of the deck. She fell through the hatch that I had left open. It was about a six-foot drop, and as she fell, I tried to catch her, but it happened so fast that I was only able to slow down the inevitable. We eventually got her out of the engine room, onto the deck, and called an ambulance to take her to the hospital. The x-rays showed that she had a badly sprained ankle. Thank God that it was not broken, but this event was just another instance of Dinny's desire to be by my side, even though it physically hurt her to do so.

We were often interviewed on television on the topic of our success with "The Miss Majestic" and the lake. One day, we had a bunch of state officials on the boat for a fishing trip. Local television reporters caught Virginia by surprise and asked her some questions while on camera. She did quite well until they asked her some technical questions about the fish. She tried to fake it and mentioned something about all of the different species of fish in the lake. It was funny for us to watch, and she was good naturedly "razzed" about it for years. She was such a good sport!

Perhaps the most frightening experience that Dinny and I shared during our marriage occurred when we owned three boats – a 72-foot party boat, a

40-foot fishing boat and a 30-foot fishing boat. Well, one fall day, when we were about to end our season, I had to go over to the marina to get the boat that my son used to run, in order to take it over to the hoist to lift it out of the water for winter storage. My wife drove my truck over to Riverside Marina to meet me and to help with the dock lines. This boat had a single propeller, and when I was backing it up, it went to the left because of the pitch of the prop. As I drove the boat over there, Virginia was standing on what we call a "finger dock." It is a dock that just sticks out in the river from the main dock. As I backed the boat into the dock, the stern came close to the end of the dock on which Dinny was standing. She bent over to push the boat away but I did not see her. At that time, I gunned the engine ahead at the same time that my wife pushed the stern. As a result, she fell forward and grabbed the stern of the boat. All of a sudden, I heard her scream, so I looked back. There she was hanging onto the back of the boat. I, instantly, ran to the stern of the boat in order to lift her out of the water, but I could not do it. I could not back up, for fear of getting her legs tangled up in the propeller. I could not go forward, for fear that she would fall off the boat. Remember, she could not swim! By that time, we were out in the river about thirty feet away from the dock. I took a life ring back to her, but she would not let go of the boat. I was about to throw a line around her, when, thankfully, the wind drifted the boat back to the dock. Some people, who were on the dock, came running as the boat got closer to them and helped me to get Virginia back up on the dock. For over a month, I was a total wreck, as I imagined her falling off that boat and drowning. Remember, she could not swim!

From these little anecdotes, I hope you can see what an amazing woman Virginia Jaycox was. She was humble, faithful, beautiful, loving, and generous to a fault. She was my wife, the mother of our children, my helpmate, and foremost the love of my life. What man could ask for more than she gave to me over the sixty years of marital bliss.

MY BELOVED

Dinny working on nets

Dinny and me on Vacation

We celebrated "The Miss"   *Dinny and me with Carol*

Our son, Bobby, and Dinny   Beautiful Virginia and Carol

Virginia in the Florida sun   Dinny with a nice fish

The Betty-J with sides off for Charters

The Miss Majestic

RITA'S STORY

I was born in Lorain, Ohio in 1925, two years before Virginia, and we were more than sisters; we were best friends, keeping each other's secrets and sharing each other's hopes and dreams. Life in those days was really quite difficult, and very different from today. This Recession is nothing compared to the impoverishment we had to suffer during the Depression. Dinny and I had to sleep with our brother, Bill, in the same bed for years; no one ever got to have his or her own bed – there wasn't room for ten beds in our house to accommodate all of us kids and our parents, so we trebled up.

Our mother baked her own bread, and when she ran out of flour or yeast, she walked ten blocks to the bakery for day-old bread, if she had the money to buy it. We were so poor that we qualified for the large wheels of government cheese, and survived on that by scraping off the mold. I remember eating a lot of kidney stew, because it was very cheap to buy and very filling to eat. The biggest drawback to that meal was the smell of urine that clung to the house for days after, because of the need to boil the organ for such a long time.

Because we were devout Catholics as young people, she and I walked to church several times a week. If the weather was bad, we went to St. Stan's on 28th Street, six blocks away, but when the sun shone, and it was nice outside, we walked to St. Joe's, seventeen blocks away from our home. I remember one day in church when Virginia and I got to laughing over something silly, and as a result an usher had to escort us out. We both were mortified! Church was a place of serenity and quiet, not a place for two girls to have a laugh fest.

As kids, we played baseball in the street all of the time, because there was no traffic; no one could afford a car in our neighborhood. The only other girl in our area was Charlotte Springowski, so the three of us spent hours playing hopscotch on the sidewalk. We also loved going to the movies, so we went to the Italian bakery on Broadway to buy bread to eat at the Elvira Theater, just down the block from the bakery. The place was so infested with rats that we had to hold our feet up while watching the movie, so as not to be bitten. When we were old enough, Dinny and I often went roller skating. That was about the time that she and I went to work at American Stove. It was right after our mother died, and whatever money we made, we gave to our older sister, Van, who took care of the household management. At work, I tore paper, while Virginia built stoves. One day, this red head, Dorothy, decided to knock all of Dinny's stoves over, which made her cry. I was so angry that I went after Dorothy, got her down on the floor, punched her, and bounced her head off of the floor, using handfuls of her hair. In those days, if there was a problem with workers, many companies held courts with workers presiding. All three of us were given a three-day furlough. As a result, our sister, Van had a fit and asked what were we going to do for food? Obviously, we survived the furlough.

Virginia was a shy, reserved teenager with little or no self esteem. When boys asked her to roller skate with them, she laughed in their faces. But, as fate would have it, it was at the roller rink where she met Bob Jaycox, her first and only love. He had asked her for a date, but she was too timid to go out with him at that time. He was so persistent that she finally relented, and they were eventually married. Dinny was an excellent wife and mother. She was a bit over protective, and some would say that she spoiled them rotten, but she did not care! They were her children, and she would do what she could to make them happy, including dressing them to the "nines."

I married young, at age seventeen, and moved out of town, but over the years, I finally moved back to Lorain, and Virginia, Gertrude (our youngest sister), and I often got together for parties and coffee klatches – what we called "Bumming." We became very, very close again, often asking each for advice about husbands and kids. When Bobby and Carol, Virginia's two children, married and had children, Dinny bought everything for her grandchildren. She was so generous with her time, money, love, and spirit that it was hard to believe that a person could be so loving and caring.

As the years passed, and she became ill and lost so much weight, I asked her to please get help to find out what was the matter, but she refused. Finally in 2007, she gave in and the rest you know from earlier in this book. I was so hopeful that this procedure would work, and that once again she would be healthy and stay that way. I was at the hospital on the day of the surgery. She looked good afterwards when I was able to visit her. I told her to be careful and not to take too much medication from the morphine pump, because it had made me nauseated when I had had my procedures two years earlier. My grand daughter-in-law took me to visit her the next day, and she seemed to be on the mend. Then disaster struck, and she was gone. I grieved and still grieve over her. She was my "Bumming Pal." Now there are only two of us left out of nine – Evangeline and me – and we are in our eighties, so only the Lord knows how long we are left on this earth.

CAROL'S STORY

September 15, 2007 will forever be engrained in my mind. It was clearly the worst day of my life. It was the day that my mother -- my best friend – died. I remember walking out of the hospital, pushing my dad in the wheelchair, knowing from that moment on, our lives had just forever changed. What an empty, horrible feeling it was; I'll never forget it! I still feel the numbness, and it's been almost nineteen months since her passing. Nothing is the same without her – nothing!

I often wonder why my bond with my mom was so tight. How can a person love someone so much that her heart actually hurts because I miss her so? That is how I explain my pain – my heart just hurts. One might think that it is impossible, but it sure is. The bad thing is that I think one must have to experience it before one can understand what I mean.

I was born August 27, 1958. There is a span of ten years between my brother and me. There were only two of us. I know that my brother grew up with my mom pretty much being there for him one hundred percent of the time, while my dad worked – sometimes two jobs at a time. I think that my brother and my mom shared a different bond than my mom and I had. I think a daughter's relationship with her mom is much different than that of a son's.

I remember that when we got into discussions, or talked to others and got on the subject of me, my mom always described me as a quiet, shy little girl. When I was little, she could set me in the middle of a room, and she could leave the room. When she came back, there I was in the same spot! I guess she could put me down, and there I'd stay! She told people that all the time. She always said what a good kid I was.

Growing up, she used to love to curl my hair. Starting at about three years old, I had hair like Shirley Temple, growing up. Every night, or there about, I sat on the floor in our living room on West Erie Avenue, while she rolled my hair up in curlers. I always had long hair, and I managed to get snarls really easily, and she sat for hours, combing out my snarls, and tugging on my head. She called them "rats' nests!" While that I sat there, I watched either the Ed Sullivan Show, or Sonny and Cher, who were my idols growing up. Anyways, by the time that my mom was done rolling my hair, and getting the snarls out, I was so mad at her for hurting me and tugging so hard. I also remember being angry because sometimes the curlers were so darn tight that my head hurt, or my eyes looked like a Chinese girl's, because those curlers were so tight!!!! Oh, what I would give to have her here today to curl my hair. I would not mind a bit. What a great thing that it would be, to have her back. I miss her so!

While I was growing up – maybe from fourteen years old – my mom worked in our fish store. She and my dad had a store near Fourteenth Street and Broadway that people came in to buy fresh fish. It was called J & J Fish. She was home for me in the morning before I went to school, but when I came home, I had the house all to myself. I always cleaned the house for her, and sometimes I surprised my parents and had supper ready. That was such a treat for her! I loved hearing her come in the door so pooped from filleting fish all day and being on her feet, to be able to sit down to eat. She was a hard, hard worker. She worked like a man, but she wouldn't have had it any other way. She was by my dad's side, every step of the way. She'd have it no other way.

In the summertime, she left notes by my bed, telling me to have a good day, and to enjoy myself. She always left a couple of dollars to go downtown and to enjoy a soda with my friends. She forever made me feel so loved. She loved the fishing business, and it gave our family a nice lifestyle that was very comfortable growing up. We were not rich, but we were very comfortable, and always had nice things.

Christmas time was always our special time of the year. Growing up as a teenager, I had my own little, fake tree in my bedroom, and my mom always bought way too much for me. Every Christmas, she saved a few presents for me to open on Christmas Day, because our tradition was to open gifts on Christmas Eve. For Mom, that holiday and every holiday for that matter, was always about family. We all dressed up and went to my grandma's house, and by the time we returned home, Santa already had stopped! We opened presents, and there was always one special "big" gift for the end – that special something that I really wanted. I remember my brother having to take me to wait either on the steps leading to our basement, or to our upstairs. I was able to hear the "Ho! Ho! Ho's!" of Santa coming into the house. Then we were called back into the room, and there was the present that I always wanted! One of my most favorite was a vanity, and another, of course, was a three-speed bike with a banana seat! I took it outside, and rode that bike in the snow. It was really neat remembering how great it felt to switch gears for the first time!

Our annual family vacation destination was Miami Beach, Florida. During the day, my dad and brother went fishing, while Mom took me to the pool at the Ocean Shores Motel, right there on the strip. I was a water bug, and I still am! We spent hours upon hours there, and she never came into the water. She sat and just watched me, never saying, "Let's go, or hurry up, or are you done yet?" She was very patient, and always so caring. She liked the hot weather, but she just never swam. She really did not know how to swim,

really. All of her life, she went on the lake and ocean with my dad, and never knew how to swim, nor did she care to know. Maybe it had something to do with her hair, because she had it styled on top of her head. She'd say that it was because that was the way my dad liked it.

I remember that she loved her sisters. It was always a special time when my dad worked 3 – 11 at Ohio Edison, because we got to go "bumming," as she called it. It was always time that she planned, and we were always home well before my dad got there. For some reason I think she thought he had no idea that we did that, but I think that he really did know. I remember going over to Aunt Gert's house on West 36th Street, where I played games with my cousin, Sharon. It is still a joke today with Sharon that once my mom yelled upstairs to tell me it was time to go home, Sharon made me help clean up and to put the games away with her. I never left her house without doing so! Aunt Gert used to play the organ, and she always played a special Halloween song for me that I loved. She had three children – Sandy, Carl, and Sharon, who was the youngest, so she was stuck with me. We have always been close. Mom sat and talked for hours to Aunt Gert, who died at a young age, and my mom was heart-broken after that.

There is also Aunt Rita, whom I remember lived on East Erie in a big house. We went there so that Aunt Rita could do Mom's hair, or my cousin,

Connie did it sometimes. She always had high, high hairdos, like a bird's nest, or all curls up on top of her head. She always wore babushkas, once her hair was done. She'd put two cans of hairspray on it to keep it in place. My dad loved my mom's hair long, so she never cut it. It was long for as long as I can remember. Oh, my gosh! If we had stock in cans of Hairnet Hairspray, today we'd be rich! She also wrapped turbans around her head at night sometimes, when her hairdo was newer, so she would not mess it up when she slept!

There is also Aunt Van, whom we'd go over to visit on the East Side of Lorain, along with Uncle Marion. When we were there visiting, I went outside to practice my cheerleading as a young girl! That was how we usually spent our time together, or going to one of my brother's baseball games.

As I grew older, we loved to shop. On payday, my mom took me and spent money on me at the mall. She never, ever spent any money on herself. That is why she went to my aunt's to have her hair done. I was always a well dressed kid growing up in junior and senior high school. I'll never forget the very first leather coat that my mom bought me at the mall. She put it on layaway, and was so proud when she got it out, and I wore it.

When I was dating Mike, who is now my husband, she let him come along on a Sunday, out to the mall with us. She treated us to lunch at the Harvest House Restaurant that used to be there at the mall. It was such a treat for all of us! He looked forward to that on a Sunday, or he looked forward to mom's home-cooked meals on Sundays. He ran over from his house on Washington Avenue, jumped the school fence, and "hightailed" it into our house, as the meal was usually on the table waiting for him. Some of her best dishes were her roasts and mashed potatoes, or baked chicken. The house always had a wonderful aroma of food!

When I got older and married, it was tough on my mom not to have me in the house, even though we only lived two doors away, because I still was not in the room across from her. She eventually became accustomed to it. When I became pregnant with Nicole, she came over one day and told me that once I had my own child, I would not need her as much. I told her, "Bologna! I'll need you even more." I'll never forget that I was due, in early April, and was two weeks past my due date. She and Mike took me to my doctor's appointment. I was large, and sick of wearing my winter maternity clothes, and was not about to buy new. The weather was starting to turn warm. Anyways, the doctor examined me, and told me that he thought that I had at least another week or so to wait. I stormed out of that office, mad at the world. I wanted that baby out!!! Mike asked my mom to take me home, while he went over to his dad's house, as he used to do every Saturday to help him with the lawn and to have a few beers. As she drove me home, I was pouting, and miserable. I told her that I wanted to go home to bed. This was the Saturday before Easter Sunday – April 21, 1984. I went home, went to bed, and cried myself to sleep for the afternoon. When I awakened, I called my mom to ask her to take me to Faroh's for some chocolate. She, of course, agreed to do it. By the time that we returned home, I was not feeling really well. I was having cramps, or so I thought, because they were not severe or anything too unusual. Mom talked me into coming over to her house, while she prepared the Easter meal for the next day. I sat in her kitchen for hours, talking to her. In between doing things, she said, "Let's go for a walk." She swore that by walking, if a woman was in labor, that gravity brought the baby down the birth canal. Little did I know that she was right! This had been going on since about 3:00 in the afternoon. By dark, we were not walking outside anymore. I was swiftly walking around her dining room table. Mike still was not at home by 8:30 in the evening. At 8:45, he called to tell me that he was home. Mom answered the phone and told him that he better come over, that she thought that I was in labor. I was not in the horrible pain that television portrays. I really was not all that sure that it was labor. When he left his father's, the last thing his dad said was, "Don't call me tonight to say that Carol's in labor." Well guess what? At about 9:45 that night, Mike brought the Mazda around to the front of my mom's house, and in that little car we went – Mom, Mike, and me. We arrived at the hospital, and at 11:35, a little girl was born, who has enhanced all of our lives. My parents were right outside the labor room and were able to hear me let out one yell. Then they got to see Nicole in her little basket as they rolled her down the hall to the baby nursery. From then on, Mom was there always to lend a hand.

A few months later, little did we know that she was walking around with uterine cancer. She had all of the tell-tale symptoms, and her doctor kept telling her that she just had an infection. I got her in to see my physician who referred her to a specialist, who determined that it was, in fact, uterine cancer. That was scary! She was in her fifties by then, and she courageously went through a radium implant into her uterus for three days, and then experienced a hysterectomy, followed by radiation therapy. She pulled through with flying colors, and remained cancer free for the rest of her life.

I shall fast forward to her last year with us, because that is what I remember so vividly, unfortunately. Mom went from two hundred pounds to 117. We finally talked her into going into a major metropolitan hospital, as that was our best bet, we thought, for her survival of this rapid weight loss. We got her a wonderful doctor who was compassionate and knew what he was doing. He inserted a lead into the main artery of her heart, and I learned how to administer TPN – Total Protein Nutrition. I went to her house at night and hooked her up to this "bag of goodies," we called it. She was connected for twelve hours at night, and in the morning I stopped by to disconnect her. I loved doing that for her! Finally, I felt as though I could pay her back for all of the times that she was there for me! She looked forward to me coming over. This procedure began in May, 2007, and I kept up this routine, day in and day out until mid June. My dad watched me care for my mom, and wanted to learn how to do it. First he learned to disconnect her for me, so that it saved me from going over in the morning. Then he learned how to administer the vitamins, complete other procedures, and to hook her up at night. He did this so that I could go on vacation with my family. I think they thought that they were holding me back from our family vacation that we usually took to Myrtle

Beach each year. Well, we decided not to go anywhere until late August. I ended up not spending my birthday at home with family. For the first time in my life, we didn't have a family gathering; we were in Fort Myers, Florida, vacationing. We returned from there, and I had to do some travel for work. On Wednesday, September 12th, Mom went into the hospital for surgery. She never came home. The haunting thing is that she told us when we saw her alive, on the 14th, we walked into her room, and she was disoriented. The first thing she said was, "I am not coming home." She did not come home to her house, but she did go to the Lord's house. I firmly believe that she is now an angel. The lady loved angels; she had a thing for angels, and she is now one, of that, I am certain.

*   *   *   *

PENNIES FROM HEAVEN

I have a story to tell you, and you may think that I am nuts, but I don't think so. What I am about to tell you, brings hope to anyone who has lost some one and feels that their heart hurts. Here it goes …

Back when Mike's dad was alive, he and I made bets on football games, basketball games, or anything to harass each other. Anyway, Mike's dad passed away before I could repay him some of the money from the bets that I had lost. While he was alive, I bought funny cards and taped a few pennies inside the card and mailed them to him. He'd call me at work, and when I answered he'd say, "This is Guido, and Gene told me that if you don't pay him the money you owe him … you'll be sorry." You get the picture … it was a fun thing. After he died, I told Mike that I should have put a bag of pennies into his casket, but I didn't. It was very shortly, thereafter, that I was on a business trip to Michigan. I made a stop at a Cracker Barrel to use the restroom. A lady with a walker was in front of me, and she bent down in the doorway and was trying to pick up something. She could not reach it, so I got it for her. When I went to give it to her, she said, "No, it's yours to keep." I did not think a thing of it. That very same day, when I checked into my hotel room, I pulled back the covers to the bed that night. There on my mattress by my pillow was a shiny penny, heads up. Again I did not think a thing of it. The next day I went to my meeting, and went to lunch. As I was walking into the restaurant, I found another penny. It was at lunch that I mentioned all of the pennies that I was finding and how odd it was. My friend from Michigan said, "Carol, didn't you and your father-in-law have something going with pennies?" It was at that moment that I began wondering if it was some kind of signal from him.

Weeks passed and nothing – no pennies. Then when I was worried about something or concerned about finances, or something, I found a penny, always, always, heads up. This is important to note! It became something that I knew was Mike's dad. Every time that I found a penny from then on, my worries were for nothing. It always seemed to turn out that way. So it came to be that when I found a penny, I became instantly happy. I saved the pennies, always. I ended up telling others, and they, too, subsequently found pennies. We seemed to think that it was a way for us to feel good and to have hope!

When my mom died, I put a little box in her casket with her. It was something she wore around her neck all of the time, and she'd put money in it, as well as her driver's license. It got so that she never carried a purse, only this goofy-looking box thing that she wore around her neck. Anyway, the last morning before we buried her, when I got to the funeral home, I put a penny in that box that she wore around her neck. I whispered to her, "Send me a penny, but make it tails up, and I'll know that it is you."

I kid you not, until this day, my family and I find pennies. About ninety-eight percent of the pennies that I now find are always tails up. There are hardly ever heads up pennies anymore. When any of us finds pennies, and we do, in the oddest of places and hardly coincidentally, we invariably always feel happier, and sense that it is she …

You may choose not to believe; that is okay. We all need something to hang on to, and I guess this is it, for our family. There is also a poem, which is to be found in another chapter of this book; it is called "Pennies from Heaven," and it says that when an angel misses she tosses down a penny! Sheer coincidence – I don't think so.

There is not a day that goes by that my dad and I don't talk. You know what they say, that out of something bad, comes something good. And all that I can say is that I know my dad has always loved me, but now we share a deeper bond, one that we wished that we had never shared – and that's seeing her the night before she died and the morning of her passing. It haunts us and always will. Every time that we get together, our conversations turns to the lady who touched our lives so very deeply that we will never, ever forget her – not even for one day. Yet that day brought us ever so much closer. Now, we look to the heavens and talk to her and tell her that we love her so. Someday we will all be together again …

Carol

Our special times together

My Mother doting on my daughter, Nicole

A FEW OF HER FAVORITE THINGS

Things she loved the most – Family

Holiday – Christmas and Birthdays

Songs – Louis Armstrong's, "What a Wonderful World, and Rod Stewart's, "Have I told You Lately That I Love You?"

Color – Purple

Fears – bugs and water

Food – Arby's apple pies, Egg rolls, really anything; she loved to eat and to eat out.

Vacations – Miami Beach

Television – The Lifetime Channel and Mystery movies

Most Proud of – Grandchildren

Collected – Angel statues, Angel pins, anything with Angels

Zodiac Sign – Taurus, the Bull

Favorite Charity – Children's Indian Village, St. Jude Children's Hospital, Veterans Association.

VAN'S STORY

This is very difficult for me to write because our sister, Virginia, was a most precious and beautiful girl. As children, growing up was very hard for us, because our family was very poor. Although our dad had a very good business, the Depression years were very difficult for many families in Lorain. There was Billy, Rita, Virginia, Gertrude, me (Evangeline), and Mom and Dad. Food was hard to come by, and we went to bed hungry many a night. How our mom did it to raise all of us kids, I will never know. We all had our chores to do, and we did them without question. Our mother was very strict. We all went to Saint Joseph Church on 15th Street, which is nineteen blocks from where we lived on Thirty-Fourth Street. Summer and winter, we walked it. Being strict Catholics, we attended mass daily. Walking to school was awful. The deep snow, in those days, made walking impossible, but we had to do it. We would stop at any opened store along the way to get warm, then continued on. We all looked after each other.

When our mother passed away in 1945, I was married at that time, so I moved home to help to keep the family together. I recall that we used to charge our food at a store, called Sol Dins. We would pay him when we could. It was hard, but people like he was had a big heart, and trusted us. We were very happy, and as we did dishes, we would sing together and laugh. We had good times and bad, but we almost always made the best of them.

Virginia was my best friend and helped out all of the time. She was a loving and caring person. She finally met and Carol. She watched over her kids like a mother hen. As grand kids showed up, Virginia was there to spoil them. She and Bob became inseparable and enjoyed a happy and lasting marriage of over sixty years.

I often called her on the phone to speak with her about her health. She played the subject down, and worried about everyone else. She suffered for so long and so much, it seemed as though the doctors could not find the trouble. When she finally went to the hospital, the operation was a success, but she passed away. We were all devastated, and our hearts were broken. I thank God for the wonderful years that we had with our sister, Virginia, and we pray that she is in God's hands.

I am now eighty-eight years old and look forward to seeing Dinny someday soon.

Love,

Van

BOBBY'S STORY

A book is not big enough to hold all of the thoughts I have for my mother. Her loss was a stab in the heart to all of us in this family.

Mom was not just a Mom, but a friend. Anyone could talk to her about anything. Most of all she was a real buddy. She always had time for me. When Mom was five months pregnant with my sister, Carol, she was chasing baseballs at Lake View Park for me. Never in sixteen years, did she miss anything I did – baseball, basketball, or track. Even in Boot Camp, Mom and Dad came to see me. Words can not say what a terrific mother she was. She was an angel. Our home was full of angels, but she was the real one! I can hear her say, "You're gonna miss me when I'm gone." I always smiled and said, "Where are you going?" Well, wow! Was she ever right! Not a day goes by that I don't cry or tell her how much I love and miss her.

My biggest regret is that I never got to give her that last hug or kiss goodbye. This is so hard! I am crying while I write this. I can honestly say that it does not get any easier. I miss her so much! I feel so all alone. My mother was my backbone; she was my reason for waking up in the morning. It seems like yesterday that Mom and I were out to eat. Mom loved that! We always could not wait for Dad to go out on the lake so that we could go to Chris's Restaurant. Mom is not just a word, she was a way of life. She was perfect in any way. I only hope and pray that God will share his kingdom with me, so that I can see my mom. I can honestly say that I am not afraid of death, just knowing that I will see my mom. It is so hard to believe that she's not here. When I go to my parents' house, I still look for her to come around the corner and say, "Oh, Bobby's here!" I am fifty-eight years old, and I am still her Bobby. There is so much that I miss about Mom, because she was so terrific. I will forever love my mother more than life itself. She was what Moms are all about. Everything that she did, she did for others. She was a mother to us all, never asking for anything for herself. If I had a toothache, she was there. If I had a bad day, she was there. She was the backbone of this family, and we all miss her deeply. God bless you, Mom. I love and miss you.

Bobby

Bobby And Dinny

GRIEF'S STORY ... A DIARY

At Three Months ...

After we buried our beautiful Virginia, I began to engage in introspection on love, life, death, grief, and religion. When a person loses someone close, and death takes away a loved one, life takes on a whole new meaning, or no meaning at all. Things that were so important to me, suddenly became insignificant. Tears come from nowhere; the uncontrollable crying consumes me. My friends do not understand. They try to remind me of the good times that I shared with my loved one. It all seems like a bad dream. I hope that somehow this will all disappear, and tomorrow I will wake up, and my lovely Dinny will be there next to me. Life seems so empty now. I try to put my mind at ease and look for something to do that will take away the sick feelings in my stomach and in my heart. Nothing seems to work. My thoughts are a tangle of questions: Where is she now? How is she now? I put flowers on her grave. I purchased the beautiful head stone with her name shining brightly in brass. Daily I visit the grave and weep over her buried body. It's been three months now, and I wonder how long this emptiness will last.

People who seem to know say that the softening of my grief will take time. Some say that my wife, in reality, died ten years ago, but I still have problems with it. Hearing that tells me that I am committed to suffering with this angel on my mind forever. My daily crying spells come and go, depending on my mood. At this point, I see no need to remove her clothes, to sell the house, or to change anything. Virginia loved this house, and she loved me – that did not change because she died. I look for every signal that she might be near. As many of my friends and those who knew her have repeatedly told me, "She is an angel sitting on your shoulder," and I believe it, because she had our home full of angels in the forms of pictures and knick-knacks. One day my daughter came over to the house, sat, and talked with me. I told her about a penny that was sitting on the kitchen table. She picked it up and put it in a jar that Dinny had used for saving change. The next day, I came downstairs, and there sat another penny in the same place. I picked it up and put it in the jar with the other pennies. I went over to my wife's desk and started to pick up some papers there, sorting through them. One sheet dropped out of the sheaf and fell to the floor. I paid no attention to it and removed some papers to throw away. I returned to the dining room, near my wife's desk and noticed the paper that I had dropped. I bent over to pick it up, and here is what it said:

PENNIES FROM HEAVEN
I found a penny today,
just laying on the ground.
But it is not just a penny,
this little coin I found.
Found pennies come from heaven,
that's what my Nana told me.
She said angels toss them down,
oh, how I loved that story.
She said when an angel misses you,
they toss a penny down.
Sometimes just to cheer you up,
make a smile out of your frown.
So don't pass by that penny,
when you're feeling blue.
It may be a penny from heaven,
that an angel's tossed to you.

The "Pennies from Heaven" thing, at first seemed to be just a coincidence, and as time passed, we all, in our family, had a strange feeling that it was not just a coincidence.

My daughter, Carol, came over to the house, one day about two months or so after my wife's death, and asked me if I felt like getting rid of her mother's clothes, maybe to give them to the Salvation Army, or to someone in need. I told her, "No, Carol, I'm not ready for that yet." She said, "Okay, but how about her shoes? Mom had about twenty pairs of shoes, and some are brand new and still in their boxes. Why not give them to someone?" I told her to go ahead and give them away, but that she might want to keep the newer ones. She said, "By the way, Dad, I'm kind of hurt that Mom has not sent me any pennies." She left to go home. About an hour later, she called, all excited, and asked me to guess what had happened? When I asked, "What," she told me that when she returned home, she opened a box of shoes and took out the paper stuffing, and out came a penny from the toe of the shoe. From then on, we began to find pennies in some very strange places. After about five months of this, we were convinced that the pennies were from heaven.

I had been suffering so badly from the loss of Virginia that my family and friends convinced me to take a cruise to get away. I called my son, and we flew down to Fort Lauderdale, Florida to take that cruise to the Bahamas. We boarded the ship and were led to a stateroom which was very small. As we sat there, disappointed and heartsick, we decided to get off the ship and to forget the trip. As we were leaving, the manager of the liner spotted us and asked where we were going. We explained that we did not like the accommodations and decided to leave. He saw my Navy hat and asked if I was a Navy man. I told him that I had served in the Navy during World War II and that my son was a Vietnam vet. He said, "Hold on! I will get you a better room." He returned a few minutes later and asked us to follow him. He ushered us into a beautiful stateroom with a large port light overview of the Atlantic Ocean. As he left, we thanked him, and to put our bags down to open them to put our things away. My son, Bobby, said, "Dad?" I answered with a "what." He found not one, not three, just two pennies. Were they put there? Did they fall there? Why were we taken to that stateroom? The Lord works in mysterious ways. It made us happy, and I'm sure that it made Dinny happy. Now we felt a lot closer to her as we tried to get through this painful part of our lives. Now I am beginning to thank God for giving me sixty years with this wonderful woman, for he truly gave me an angel.

The days fly. Time has no meaning for me anymore. Each night, when I go to bed, I pull the covers back and tell my wife that it is another day closer to the day when we will meet again in heaven.

At Six Months ...

Though it is six months now since my Dinny died, it seems like twenty years ago. I try to see her in my dreams and fail to see her face. The warm, beautiful lady with whom I shared my bed, is now laying in a cold, drab grave in the cemetery. It seems like my life has become one long memory of pain and sorrow. When I attempt to remember all of the wonderful times that we had together, my thoughts often wander back to my pain and sorrow.

The one thing that I find, now that I have had time to think openly about my wife's death – is it a religious awakening? Where is she? How is she? Is she an angel now? If so, I wonder what she is doing. Is she happy? Is she with her mother, father, sisters, and brothers, who have gone a long time ago? I am not a church-goer, and some might say that I am selfish, yet I have been one who will help anyone in need, if he or she tries to help him- or herself first. Some people seem to go through life in one crisis after the other and need help badly. I now feel the need to carry on the donations to the various agencies that my wife so unselfishly gave money. I sent a check to the Indian Reservation School out West, along with a picture of Virginia, and informed them of her death. I did the same thing with the four or five other organizations that Dinny felt the need to help. That big jar that she filled with pennies now contains all of the pennies that I have found. Soon, I will take that jar to the bank and make out a few checks for the charities she loved from the proceeds of those pennies.

I cried so much and for so long as my grief consumed me that my daughter insisted that I go to the doctor to seek help. I did, so he prescribed some pills for me to take. As anyone, who is over seventy years old knows, we generally take lots of pills. Virginia's pill box was loaded with pink ones, grey ones, and white ones. I really did not want any more pills, so I got to thinking. God meant for us to feel the pain and sorrow that is built into our hearts, so I did not take the pills that were supposed to end my crying and sorrow. I cry now, when I feel like it, and I feel no shame, as this is not a bad thing to do. We are going to miss and to cry at the loss of our loved ones. Time may slow the tears, but I don't think it will ever dull the hurt. The one thing that really crosses my mind is the religious part of a death in the family – how can one help but to ask what is happening to one's loved one after death. I do not care how religious a person is, these questions come to light as he or she seeks answers.

My friends and family told me to go to see a reverend or a priest to seek solace and to receive a better knowledge of the Lord's Bible. I had an opportunity to visit with a local pastor of a church here in Lorain, Ohio, to whom I posed these very questions. He made every effort to find the answers for me. One question I offered to him was: when I die, and hopefully to go heaven, will I see my wife again, and how will she look? His answer was, "She will not look as you have known her, but you will recognize her right away. I asked him the one question that confuses me: when death occurs where do we go? Do we all go to a place and stay until Judgment Day? Are we all raised or lowered at once, or do we go to Purgatory and are judged right away to enter heaven or go to hell? He sort of dodged that one, as he kind of changed the subject by quoting parts of the Bible. I did not understand. I have tried to read the Bible, but found it too confusing to understand. I believe in Jesus Christ, and I strongly believe in our Lord, but I wonder sometimes, why are we here? The only thing that I can come up with is that we are in hell now, and our performance here decides where we end up. I recall parts of the Bible where Jesus was on the cross, and one of his disciples on the cross next to Him asked, "Remember me." So he had faith in Jesus and was raised to an everlasting life. So I asked the reverend, "Why must we forget our natural born instinct to have the inquisitive nature that God gave us? Why is death so secret?" I felt guilty asking these questions, as I love God and hope someday to be at His side, along with my wife. I wonder in my heart of hearts, if others have the same questions. It doesn't make a person an unbeliever to ask this, or does it? The confusion is magnified by the different religious views of others. Jews believe in Jesus, but do not recognize him as the Son of God. I always thought that the Jews were God's chosen people. How could they denounce His Son, Jesus? It gets more confusing when I look at other religious faiths, but the one faith that really makes me wonder is Islam. Their God is Allah, and their beliefs are much different than ours about death. I respect all religions, because they contribute to a better understanding of life itself. Who is right or wrong? No one knows, but faith can move mountains, and it seems that mankind has to believe in something. So with that in mind, any religion is better than none.

There is no way that we can look at life and not see our Maker behind our earth and life. All are tied together – the sky, the wind, the birds, the bees, the trees, the flowers, the grass, the sea and the ocean. All depend on each other. This did not just happen. The Lord, our Maker, put it here. We are His children, and we will be judged; of that I am certain. I do believe that Jesus walked the earth and was the Son of God. He died on the cross for our sins. I do not understand the why and the how; I just do not know. The Lord could have programmed us all to be good. I believe that he wanted us to make that choice. I believe that here on earth, we are doing just that. I believe that death will come as a big shock to some. I also believe that the outcome may not be what we had intended, or it is possible that when we die, we may never wake up. Who knows? Maybe the Bible tells us, but I do not understand it well enough to say. I wonder if any of us does. The interpretation is open to question. Only time will tell. My wife knows; I am certain. It is ironic, though that I always feared death, but now I find myself asking God to take me to my wife. How quickly life changes one's agenda and outlook. My possessions now mean nothing to me. Maybe, just maybe, later on, they will, but I am 82 years old, so I don't see that happening.

Life is full of pain, sorrow, and setbacks, but nothing compares with the loss of a loved one who is close to one's heart, like a wife or a mother. I often wondered how some people handle this kind of loss. As we explore this dark, deep shadow of death, I am sure that everyone has a different way of looking for and asking questions about the hereafter. I have so many questions about my wife's death. To begin with, she died in a major hospital under questionable circumstances. She had been plagued with painful illnesses for the past fifteen years. Each time she entered the hospital for an operation, we became more and more complacent about her recovery. So when her last surgery occurred, we never dreamed the worst would happen. Her death left a hole in our family's hearts, and caught us totally by surprise. I am sure many of you who read this book have experienced the same feeling. It gnaws at me day in and day out. Why? Why? Why? She died in a hospital where that should never have happened. At first my heart was broken and sad. As time passes, I began to get angry and bitter. Why didn't they watch her better? Her death should never have occurred. At one point, I engaged an attorney to seek out the answers for her death. I found that lawyers do not like long and expensive fights, so they shy away from suing a major hospital in favor of easier cases that take less time and money. Hospitals know that, and in many cases, get away with malpractice. This book is not dedicated to that pursuit. It is meant to ask and to answer some of the questions about our lives here on earth and our eventual deaths. We will explore the various major religious beliefs regarding life after death. Hopefully we can come up with a better understanding of death: where we go, and what may lie ahead for us and for our loved ones.

Many of us have read the Bible, and I am certain that we have, at one time or another had a hard time understanding the Word of God as written there. I tried to read sections of it to understand better how and where my wife is after her death. We, as humans, do not think much about this subject when we are young. We are trying to enjoy life, but as we age, our minds tend to bring the reality of death into a clearer, more realistic picture. Then, of course, when a person close to us dies, it really opens our eyes.

It has been six months since my wife, Virginia, died in the hospital. More than ever before I want to shout her name and to tell the world what a wonderful wife and mother she was. I always wondered why she was so attached to pictures and statues of angels. It is apparent to me now that she was preparing to meet God and to become an angel herself. She was an angel in life because she was always helping the little kids, the vets, the Army, the fire department, the police, and others who asked for donations. Once these various causes found their angel in Virginia, she was fair game. Our mail man got a long stronger hauling mail to our house, and Dinny never failed them.

She loved her family and made everyone at home in her house. Chuck and Della from Cleveland, whom we met on the Miss Majestic, our eighty passenger party boat, fell in love with Virginia. They often stopped over to our house with baked goods and things for her. Literally hundreds of people came to know her through our charter business. They would spot her in a crowd and ignore me. She was a beautiful gal with her blond hair that stuck out like a sore thumb. She was the gal who sold the tickets for the fishing trips, and I was only the captain. I didn't mind, because I was proud of her and how she handled herself.

Right at this point in my life, I have a serious back problem and am scheduled for an operation on April 9th. My wife will not be there with me this time, as she has been in the past, but I know her spirit will be with me. Our life together was one love story after another. We looked forward to each day to spend together, and now that I have lost her, I can't spend one minute without her on my mind.

And now it is seven months since my life, as I knew it, ended. It has not gotten any easier. I break down crying at any moment and try to talk to her. The medicine cabinet keeps opening up on its own; it never did that before, so I talk to it and say, "Good morning, Dinny." She never answers me, but maybe I don't hear her. I keep asking her to send me a message to say that she is okay. I look for every small thing that may be her. The pennies from heaven help.

No matter how much I write on this book, my thoughts always come back to my wife. What will happen, if for some reason I should happen to find another gal with whom to share the rest of my life? How will my wife feel about that? Will it hurt her? I'm sure that every man who has lost his wife wrestles with that question. It is one decision that I don't want to make, but time heals all wounds, and I hope she understands how lonesome I am.

At Seven Months …

In two days, it will be seven months since my wife, Virginia, passed away. I am still haunted by seeing her lying there in the hospital with her eyes wide open – seeing nothing. Earlier this week I reflected on her words, "Bob, I'm not coming home this time." I ignored those words and passed them off as just that -- "words." She was, in fact, I believe saying, "Help me," but I didn't see it or hear it, and ignored her plea for help.

I have gone over and over this constant question: "How does one die in a major hospital by drowning in her own vomit? Why did I take her over there? Why didn't I take her to our local hospital? I began to blame myself and to seek various answers, but they all come out the same. She was eighty years old. It was her time to go. I do not accept this, because I say that she was a beautiful woman who looked to be only 50 years old. She should be here right now, helping me to spell these words. I know, without a doubt, that many of you reading this book, who have lost someone close to you, can identify with what I am saying. Life is such a mystery in itself, without adding death to the picture, and as hard as I try to keep religion out of the story – I cannot, for the two are so tightly intertwined – death, grief, and religion.

Every day we see where a young child of 8 or 10 years old dies of cancer, and we know the grief that must be in the hearts of the parents and loved ones of that child. We wonder how they cope with it. Life, here on earth is a beautiful thing, but it has painful roads that some people have to travel. It appears as though their entire lives experience one crisis after another. I often ask myself – why? For every wonderful and beautiful thing that we have here on earth, there are a millions others that make it ugly and cruel – war, greed, power, and death.

It is now April 20th, 2008. My back operation was a success. I have no pain at all, and there is just a small sore spot to let me know that I had surgery. It is raining out today – cloudy and dreary. Why is it that life seems so much worse when the sky is covered by the clouds, and it rains? As I start to write this morning, I look at Virginia's picture in front of me, and say, "Good morning, Punkin." "Punkin" or "Peanut" were my two pet names for her. I had to laugh, thinking back, because she rarely got mad at me, but when she did, she called me "Buster." It was almost impossible to become angry with Dinny, for she made my life a happy camper. When I went away on a long trip, taking the boat to Florida, I always wanted her to go along, but if she couldn't go, I went crazy with loneliness until I returned home to see her again. We truly loved each other and enjoyed being together. She loved to fish mostly for perch and had a feel for their bite. She always let me know when she caught the first fish, or when she hooked three at a time. She waved them in front of my face and said, "How many have you caught?" I would grasp her and give her a big hug.

The pain she experienced from her illness at home seemed to be washed away when I got her out on the boat to fish. She actually seemed to enjoy herself on the water, and it made me feel so good to see her laugh and to spend time with her. It is so hard to explain now, how I feel. At times I am bitter. Why did the Lord take her away from me? Why didn't He let her live when she was on her way to a new, painless life? Then I say to myself, how selfish of me to want to keep her here, after all of her pain and sorry. On the other hand, I think that maybe she is better off; at least I won't have to see her die an inch at a time in a home. No matter how I try to forget it, I still come back to the starting line – where is she? Is she okay? Will I see her again? Will she still love me?

Today is Monday, the 21st of April. The tulip tree near our front porch is in full bloom. It is so beautiful because its colors seem to light up the sky. Virginia used to love to see it, but many times, its flowers were short lived, as it forecasts winds and rain. Generally, we had a chance to see it for about a day before the wind shook the blossoms off the tree and on the ground. It is beautiful, but what a mess it makes. Dinny had a pretty good handle on the weather and how the seasons went. For sixty years, we watched as the seasons changed, and the tulip tree was a sign of spring for us, but we knew there was still some bad weather yet to come. Virginia always said that it won't be warm and nice until after Mother's Day. Who would have a better feeling for nice weather than a mother? "Mothers with their smiles and loving hearts can't bring anything bad," so this old saying seems to bear out this fact. Very seldom have I seen spring break out before Mother's Day. This year will be very hard on my family at Mother's Day, because the kids, grand kids, and all would be looking forward to seeing their mother and grandmother on that day.

"Grandma" or "Grandmother" has a nice ring, because it suggests pies, cookies, great food, and a gentle, loving person. Why is it that "Grandmas" never measure anything – a pinch of this or a dash of that, and there is a pie or cake that tastes so, so good and always the same. I used to love the cookies that Dinny made with peanut butter and Hershey's Kisses on top. She really got mad at me when I ate them as fast as she took them out of the oven. Then she began to hide them, but she was not too good at that. I think that you see where I am going with this. The wonderful times and a fantastic woman like Virginia can only make the greatest of memories for me. I do not know how many times that I have cried while writing this book.

Today is April 27th, 2008, my wife's birthday. I'm really in the "dumps." My sister called me from Michigan, and during our conversation, she reminded me of the date. Yes! I forgot her birthday! I felt so lousy that wanted to die. She has been on my mind constantly, but I lost track of the date.

It's five p.m., and I decided to go out and get flowers to put on her grave. I drove out to the cemetery and visited her grave. Lo and behold, my daughter had beaten me to it. There on Virginia's grave was a nice set of flowers with two balloons – one read "Happy Birthday;" the other read, "I Love You." I was so happy to see the flowers and balloons that I sat down on the grass next to the grave and asked her to forgive me. As I sat there, I thought of how close our family had been. Carol, my daughter, had been Virginia's shopping buddy as I said earlier. It was only fitting that she remembered her mother's birthday.

I actually called and thanked her for remembering. Carol had done this before she left for a business trip to Seattle, Washington. I went home and spent the rest of the day trying to explain to Virginia how I forgot her birthday.

I was never good at remembering birthdays, and always used the argument That holidays and birthdays were every day, yet now I was unable to convince myself that this was right. What I lacked in remembering, Dinny made it up doubly, for she kept a list of all the right dates and made certain that they were observed by us. She even went to far as to write my name on a gifts that I had never seen; that's the kind of person she was. In our early days of marriage, I used to buy her all sorts of gifts and hang them all over the house with signs that read, "I Love You," etc. We laughed together and cried together after the kids had grown up and moved out of the house. We became inseparable. We had each other, and no one else mattered. Now she is gone, and I have a dark cloud hanging over my head. No matter how I try, I just cannot get her out of my mind, and I do not want to do so. No one, and I mean no one, knows how painful this is, until a person actually experiences it. The passing of time does not ease the pain.

After a while I tried to make contact with her, looking for every conceivable event to tie in with her. At times I have talked to her chair, or to her, while I am driving in the car, even though I realized that it did not work. She did not answer, but I did not give up. Without thinking, my mind said that she was right there with me to talk to her, and I did.

As the days pass, I look back and wonder if this isn't all a dream? Did Virginia ever exist? It seems as though she has been gone forever, yet it has only been seven months. Then I begin to question what life has in store for my future. Will I meet up with someone else? Next, my heart kicks in and says, "How dare you even think of that? Your wife has only been gone a short time, and you want someone else already! I thought you were in love with your wife. How could you think like that?" Consequently, my lonesome self answers, "If I could just have someone to talk to. Watching television all night, alone, is not fun!" How could I bring other women into my life when I still love Virginia? Finally I conclude that this grief is going to take some time. Other questions begin to nag at me: what will Virginia feel if I did find another to share my life? What would she say? How would she feel? I do not want to hurt her. I shake my head and say, "I'm sorry, Honey. I don't want anyone but you, yet I cannot have you anymore until I die. Even then, there are no guarantees.

After all of this soul-searching my mind takes another tact. How about my wife? How is she doing? It must be harder for her than it is for me. By all indications, she can look down and see me. How devastated she must be to see me crying my eyes out and begging to be near her once again. Then my questions begin to haunt me all over again. How is she? Where is she? What does she do all day? And it goes on and on. I just cannot shake this feeling of uncertainty about the unknown. Each day I find better answers or no answers at all. I wonder how I stand with God after asking all of these questions. Aren't I supposed to have faith and believe strongly enough to get through all of this and know without a doubt that Dinny is with God in heaven, free of pain, happy with her parents and siblings. Yet, somehow, that does not seem to answer all of the questions, but it does make me feel better to believe.

But, here we go again! What if all this about God is not true? What if when you die, you're gone forever? Or, like some say, after death a person comes back as a bird or an animal? Oh my God! I don't even want to think about what could be happening to her! Of course, I know this is wrong. It can't be like that, but my mind plays tricks on me, and I have to go through all of the myths in order to get back to the truth. There is only one truth, and it is the beautiful truth – she is with God in heaven, free of pain and happy. There is no other way. God bless you, Honey. I love you dearly, and I will see you when God calls me Home.

"Good Grief!" My grandmother used to use that term all of the time, such as "Good grief! Is Paul going to be out of a job now? Or good grief, this pie is so good!" There are good griefs, but then, "Good grief! He is dead," does not make sense to me. What is good about death? In my case, Virginia and I used to talk about what would happen if one of us died. We talked back and forth on the subject and came to the conclusion that the one who died first would be the lucky one. "Good Grief," then entered my life. My wife is now in heaven and she is happily Home. Even though I have asked many questions about her fate, I know in my heart that she is safe in God's hands, and I pose these questions only to confirm what I suspect and believe. She is in my heart, on my shoulder, and in my thoughts. She's still my girl, and I will love her forever. When I pass away, I will look forward to seeing her again. At this point, I do not know what heaven will bring, but if I make it, I will grab her up and hold her tight forever. As I had always preached to her, there has to be a hereafter. Otherwise, there would be no use at all for our lives here on earth. As children, we grow up looking forward to life. As adults, we spend our lives looking forward to an everlasting life with God. So this grief we feel when our loved ones die, may indeed, be "good grief."

I am almost 82 years old now, and as I have said before, I look forward to death, because I know that I will be with Virginia. Here again, I have questions. Do they have television in heaven? Are there ball games, great restaurants, and shopping malls? What do angels do all day – pray? I don't know about you, but I enjoy all of these things here on earth and even some vices. Will heaven be boring? I don't think so. God forgives many things, and I am sure that he understands what we like. I guess it all boils down to the fact that we will not find out the answers until we die, but I will try to find answers that the Bible tries to tell us and have them explained.

I wanted to watch the Cleveland Indians play tonight, but the rain washed it away, so I figured that I may as well do some writing. Today was one of those uneventful days. I worked on my boat for a little while, then went to a restaurant for lunch. I bought lunch for a friend, returned home, and before I knew it, it was 8:30 in the evening. The Indians were sitting there in the dugout, watching it rain, just like I did.

My life has surely changed directions since my wife passed away. I have no timetable to follow, so it is not imperative that I rush home now to greet her, and as much as I grieve for her, I keep wondering how must it be for her? The things that I have experienced indicate that she is looking down on me. Our family tells me that if she is an angel or a spirit or both, that she can see us. Now, just think, if that is true, it could be just as devastating to her or to any loved one who has passed away, to see us cry and to see our pain. As spirits, are they programmed in some way that takes away that pain and makes it joy? I have spoken so many times about this unknown factor of life after death, and could it be good grief that we are seeing being returned to us by those who have passed away.

SAFELY HOME
"I am home in heaven dear ones,
Oh so happy and so bright.
There is perfect joy and beauty,
in this everlasting light.
And so the pain and grief is over,
every restless tossing passed.
I am now at peace forever,
safely home in heaven at last."

I have read that poem over and over again, and its message takes away the pain for a passing moment, as I hear my wife saying, "Bob, I'm okay. Don't worry about me. I love you still, and look forward to the day that you come and join us." I can almost hear her say that, as I concentrate on the words. If ever there was a poem that described a loved one's message from heaven, this poem, "Safely Home," can make a person feel better about a loved one's passing. It is straight forward and to the point, yet softly explains the new distance between the reader and them. It gives a person hope that you will meet again. What a beautiful way to put it!

As the months pass, I begin to understand how it feels to lose that very special person I lived with all of these years. Oh, I still talk to her. She opens my cabinet door, and I tell her good morning and tell her all about my day. I let her know about our daughter flying out to Seattle on a business trip and asked her to look over Carol. At times I feel like a fool, talking to a mirror on a cabinet. But hey, it makes me feel better that I can contact her to keep her in my mind. The days wear on me, and I long for companionship, or just have someone to talk to. I hate to admit that I may be ready for another chance at love. My conscience starts calling me every name that it can think of – you louse! My wonderful wife has only been gone now for seven months, and here I am already willing to forget her and run after another. I feel so damn rotten that I want to hide under a bed somewhere. I do not mention it to anyone because I feel too ashamed to admit it. My kids have already told me, "You're dead if you replace our mother. You keep pictures of her all around the house, plus other pieces of clothing and memorabilia to remind you that she is there with you. This helps, but you still break down and cry your eyes out for her." Even as I write this, the tears come and go. It's like she's sitting here with me, telling me to write about my feelings. I have often felt that I am not smart enough to write this book, and maybe I'm not, but I keep pecking away. It seems as though the words just keep coming. It's so easy to write about a woman like my wife. She never let me down and always lifted me up. When things went badly, she was always there for me, and here again, I am now suffering the fact of having lost the great provider who made those great meals for me every day.

I try to do what it takes to cook, but I fail miserably sometimes, but wait, there is a light at the end of the tunnel. Last evening, I decided to make pancakes for supper. I read the box, mixed up all the stuff, even broke an egg into the batter and buttered the fry pan. Believe it or not, I created a nice pair of pancakes, which I ate with joy. Before I ate them, I got out my instant camera to take pictures of pancakes which I showed to all of the girls at the restaurant. So you see, there are periods of joy as I struggle through this time of grief. Good grief or bad grief – it is all a part of life. Virginia was a beautiful person who always had a smile on her face, and when I get to feeling sorry for myself, I try to see her face smiling at me. It works most of the time to cheer me up.

As I have said before in this book, when a person has shared a bed and a life with someone, it is not easy to go it alone. Sometimes when I think if that, I get sick to my stomach. My God – how long have I got to go one like this? I have, never in my life, been alone! Then I scold myself and say, "Okay, you poor thing! Isn't that just terrible that now you have to fend for yourself with no wife to do your work for you?" I always end up telling Dinny how sorry I was that I didn't do more for her. I recall that when I came home from being out on the lake, I was pooped. She often asked me to empty the garbage can. I heard her, and had every intention to do so, but not right at the moment that she wanted. When I finally got around to it, I discovered that she had beaten me to the punch, and it was empty. She enjoyed doing things for me, and I enjoyed her. The thing that scares me right now is that she has only been gone for seven, nearly eight months, yet at times I wonder if she ever existed, and that makes me feel really low. My charter fishing business starts soon, and I hope that I can accept her death in a way that good grief prevails. I try to focus my mind on the good times that we had together and there were lots of them. Maybe as I am out on my boat with customers that I can get a glimpse of her catching a fish, laughing and enjoying life, because life without her with me in body will be tough to handle. With God's help and an angel to watch over me, I shall be okay.

As time passes into months, I miss Virginia more and more. The same old doubts linger in my head, parading slowly through my mind. I now try to concentrate on the good times that we had together, because people, whom I have talked to, advise that it is one way to ease my sorrow. I do not know why I feel so unique, like I'm the only one who has ever lost a loved one. There is no way to describe the feeling. I'm sick to my stomach; my heart aches; I feel like crying, but cannot do so. Then just when I begin to feel okay, I break down crying. Life is such a mystery, because it seems like that old saying, "Only the good die young," is true. Some of the derelicts I see walking the streets go on and on and on, yet some of the great people end up in the hospital, suffering with pain for years. How does anyone explain this? Drunks, who contribute nothing to the community, seem to go through life without much of a hitch. When I see young kids with cancer, suffering a fate that even a dog should not go through, make me wonder why God lets this happen? I realize that He does not control our lives, but it still makes me wonder.

Life after death -- where are we going; where will we end up – are questions that we have all asked; of that, I am certain. Some of us seem to believe that we have the answers. Why is it that some people accept their fates and do not question them? I sit here at this desk and wonder what I am doing here, writing about something that I know so little. This work started out as a tribute to my wife, Virginia. Bible experts are going to shoot holes in all of my words here. I should stick to what I know, and that is the grief part of my book. Isn't it ironic that I accepted death as part of life? I did not give it much thought when I was young, but as I grew older, I began to worry about my track record in life. Suddenly we become a church attendee and start to donate to local charities. We begin to remember all of the people of whom we have taken advantage. We also recognize our selfishness throughout our lifetimes and all of a sudden we try to buy our way into heaven. Now we are in our eighties, and maybe we should have started to repent a little earlier. Well this God of ours is a forgiving one, and maybe it is never too late to change. Virginia and I never went to church, but we felt that we lived a Christian life together. We prayed, and we believed in God and Jesus. Virginia's faith was unwavering. I, too believed, but I had lots of questions about the hereafter. I have always been a realist – 2 and 2 equal 4. Any term that is difficult to prove is hard for me to understand, like spirits, heaven, supernatural, and life after death. What kind of life is there in heaven? Do people there play baseball? Do they enjoy their spirit's lives and just how do they do that? After asking all of these questions, I hate to think about what will happen to me. Maybe the Lord will have me breaking rocks in a chain gang, or worse; He might send me down to see the other guy. I hope not, because I want to see my wife, my mother, and my father again, someday. Maybe He will find it in his heart to forgive me. I pray He does!

At Eight Months ...

Today, my daughter and I put flowers on her grave because it has been eight months since her passing. I used to worry about her going to the store by herself. Now my thoughts wander to where she is now. Is she okay? Is she happy? Does she miss me? I love you, Dinny, and I always will.

One of the questions I have asked many times is: when I die, and if and when I go to heaven, what will my wife look like? A pastor told me that she will be a spirit and that I will recognize her immediately. A Catholic priest said that she will look just like I saw her last. Are they both right? Could it be that as a spirit, she still remains in her physical body? Or will my eyes be adjusted to the spirit world in order to form her image? Is love still alive in heaven? Will I still carry on my love life with her, or do we all become just one happy family?

I have many more questions. Why is heaven so secret and a mystery? Why is death so final? Where is heaven? I do not doubt for one minute that this world was not created by something, but not someone. We are told that God created heaven and earth. It is hard to believe that anyone could have such powers, but when I look around me, there is no mistake. This world was created, not made. There is a big difference. Science says the world evolved into what it is today. Well, the world did a "helluva" job fitting those pieces together, all by itself. No, we did not just happen. The Guy who created this place had a plan, and we, as humans, were His major project. He gave us a brain and a body and said, "Go use it." He did not make robots. He only asked that we live by ten rules. If a person reads them, he or she will agree that they were meant to keep our lives free from pain and suffering. But it seems that mankind is not about to life up to these conditions. Greed, hate, and power have overcome love and understanding. There must be a reason why some people live by the words of God and have no trouble with it, while others choose to travel down the other road.

The great escape artist, Houdini, years ago, said that he would return from his death and let us know about it. So far, that has not happened. But I have more questions yet to be answered. Are there ghosts or spirits to whom we can talk? Many say there are, and in some cases have strong evidence that they are doing just that. Is this a case of mind reading, or do they in fact speak to the dead? As I get on with this book, I want to explore this further and interview one of these people who have the power. When my back was torturing me with tremendous pain, some of my friends told me to pray for the Lord to fix it for me. Yet the Bible tells us to seek a physician for pain. Oh yes, that's another question I have. Do you believe that people in prayer group sessions really get healed? I don't know about you, but I have held my hand up to the television screen and said a little prayer for my wife or even for myself, but it did not work. That is not to say that it doesn't, but it didn't for me or for her. Then why does it work for some? As the days turn into weeks, and the weeks turn into months, my mind starts to play tricks on me. In my case, I started to ask myself, did she ever exist? Did she die a hundred years ago? It seems that way, because I long to hear her voice. Sometimes I even call out to her, even though I know that there will be no answer. Then I say to myself, maybe if I yell louder, she will answer. I feel like a fool for doing it, but it just seems to help.

Now after saying all of this, things have happened that I cannot explain, and maybe she does hear me, but cannot answer. Let me give you an example. After Dinny's death, I had my daughter leave my wife's sweater on the towel rack over the back of the tub. The bathroom seemed to be a place where I had the feeling that Virginia was around. The medicine cabinet door, which has never come open on its own, suddenly, after Dinny's death, started to swing open, so when I took a bath, I talked to her. Well, on one occasion, my back was hurting, and I decided to take a bath. This was about eight months after she passed away. When I got in the tub, I was well clear of that sweater hanging on the towel rack at the back of the tub and had not been touched since her death. I slid down in the tub to soak my back. I was lying there for about ten minutes, when I started to talk to her. I went over many things, but when I came to, "Boy, I wish you were here in the tub with me … ," the sweater came off of that towel rack and landed on my chest. There was absolutely no reasonable way that it could fall that far forward. From that time on, I have accepted her being in my life again, and the feeling that she is with me, is stronger than ever. I then began to feel sorry for her, if she can see me. How sad that it must be not to be able to contact me to say, "I love you still."

I wonder how many people have experienced that some kind of contact from a loved one who passed away. I wish that I could include those anecdotes from people who were contacted. I just may spend a few years writing this book and have a chance to find out. I hope I do; it will be interesting to find out. When these things happen, I always try to play the "Devil's Advocate," and try to find the logical answer. Well, this last incident with the sweater blew that away! I just cannot explain it. I guess there are things in this old world that we don't understand now, but will someday, maybe!

Life is a mystery, and some experts have used a scientific approach to finding these answers, but they generally concede that they have no proof that this world of ours popped out of nowhere. When I stop to think about the people who have no belief or faith, I wonder, to what do they look forward? What motivates them into being good people who care about others? I often wondered if a study was ever done to compare atheists and their lifestyles to the lifestyles of Christians. The fact that we, as Christian, have faith and look to the heavens for everlasting life is a goal worth trying to achieve. Why would an atheist have any goals when he has no future? "Eat, drink, and be merry, for tomorrow may never come." I guess that is their philosophy. Don't get me wrong; there are plenty of Christians, who take that road, but they do have one advantage over atheists; they can ask for forgiveness.

God works in funny ways; that is for sure. Here I am writing about religion, when I know so very little about it. I can only feel that He put me up to this, and now it is my turn to learn something about myself, and maybe bring light to some of the questions that I have. I know that I am not alone when I raise these questions. A lot of people must feel the same way and must seek out these secrets to life and death.

Now that Virginia is gone, I have been asked how in the world did we stay married for so long; what was our secret? It is really quite simple. When a person falls in love with someone, she/she should try to find a common interest and spend as much time together as possible. One should make his/her spouse his/her buddy, and forget the night out with boys/girls. If a man or a woman needs to get away from his or her spouse to go out with the boys/girls, then she/he is not in love.

Virginia and I worked hard, and in twenty years, we paid off the mortgage on the boat. Working together, we accomplished our goal, and it made our marriage work. That old saying, "Behind every successful man is a great woman who made him that way," is so true, particularly in my case. It seemed like everything I did was to prove myself worthy of her. I don't want it to sound like I was the most wonderful husband in the world, because I was not. I flirted with other women, and if they flirted back, I ran. Don't ask me why, because I do not know, to tell the truth. I guess it is an ego thing with me. I was married to a beautiful woman who was a wonderful wife, and I know that my flirtations hurt her, but I always tried to make it up to her by showering her with hugs and kisses. To this day, I regret my mistakes. What a stupid thing to do, and now she is gone! I have that to live with, and it makes me sad not to be able to hold her in my arms and to say that I am sorry, Dinny, because I truly am.

Lots of times when I do things like that, I think, "Oh well, she can't see me." We forget that God can, so now I have to prove to him that I can go on and do what is right, as a remembrance to her. I have tried to continue the donations that she gave to different organizations and kind of catch myself when I use God's name in vain. I'm having a little trouble with that as my vocabulary as a sailor was kind of rough, but I am trying. Each time that I slip, I ask Him to forgive me. Years ago, I used to pray occasionally. Now, I make it a ritual, and I say a prayer every night to remind Virginia that I am one day closer to the day that I will see her again. I love life, don't get me wrong, but how much different life looks now, without her. All my valuable possessions, all my trophies, all the accolades that once seemed so important, now are just stuff that I collected along the way. It is much more important to me now to know where my wife is, and how she is.

This brings my book to another chapter, so to speak. After eight months, I am about to go crazy. The winter weather here has been atrocious, so that I have been cooped up in this house, crying and feeling sorry for myself. I do go out and buy a lunch at a restaurant, or I go to the grocery to buy food for home, but I am no cook. I live on hot chocolate and donuts, or my daughter brings over some food at times.

I try to assure myself that I will never again want another woman. Virginia will be my one and only. As the days and months pass, I long for someone to talk to, not to jump in bed with, but another buddy. Then my conscience starts to work on me. Will I hurt my loving wife of yesteryear, if I find myself in the arms of another? When I go to heaven, if I make it there, will she be there to greet me with open arms, or will she turn her back on me in disgust? I asked God to show me what to do – to show me what is right. Then I think that it is not his choice to make. It's mine. Do not think for one minute that this is not a hurdle to get over. I'm lonesome – all alone now, after spending over sixty years with a buddy. Now there is silence in my home. Her chair is empty. Her body – that beautiful, wonderful lady lies in the cemetery four miles away. I go there every chance I get, but I have mixed emotions about how I feel at her grave site. I am told that her spirit is not there. She may be sitting in my car as I visit her grave, or she may be elsewhere. Every day, I try to talk with her to share the daily news. Virginia, my love, give me some advice. If I should meet up with another woman and fall in love, what should I do? Will I hurt you? Will our love then fail? I'm lost and lonesome without you! How should I handle this? I get no answers. Life goes on, and I count each day as another day closer to the answers to my questions. It overwhelms me. My mind never quits until that pretty waitress in the restaurant smiles and tells me that she likes me. I find that my heart is still in me, and it's beating, but it is short lived because I realize that I am now 82 years old, and that poor girl is 35 or 40, at best. So my heart slows down again, and I get up and put one foot ahead of the other, as I travel toward my eventual death, down this long road of life, with no one at my side. I have no one to talk to, no one except God, and He has been there all of the time. I just did not know it. Even so, I miss her soft caresses, her gentle hugs, her wonderful laughter, and the joy of being together all of these years with her. I hope and pray that this love story never ends, and I actually look forward to death.

I am a condemned man! Every day for the rest of my life, I will feel this hurt in my heart. I can only imagine the pain that she felt after surgery and for the minutes before she choked to death on her vomit. If given the choice, I wonder what she would have chosen – a life alone, or death. As she has said many times before, "We are too close, and the one who dies first will be the lucky one." I hope and pray that she was right. All of these feelings lead me back to the questions that are still unanswered:

Where is she?

How is she?

What will she look like when I see her again?

Will she still love me?

Will our love affair still be there?

Will we be happy in heaven?

Do spirits eat?

Do they dance and play?

Is the quality of life the same, or does everlasting life get boring?

Or don't spirits get bored?

Can we still hug and kiss?

Do spirits have sex?

Hey, I can't help it. These are fair questions. God invented heaven; I did not, so why shouldn't He let us enjoy each other? If it is a sin to enjoy sex, why should He put such joy in it? Boy, there are lots of of questions to be answered, but I am sure we will eventually get all the answers we want and maybe more.

My niece, Connie Trelka, is doing some research for me on this book. She is looking into all of the different major religions to see what their beliefs are regarding the hereafter. If any of you reading this book have been there and have returned to this life, I would love talking to you.

We all believe in angels, and I know my wife is one now, but what does an angel do all day? Does she fly around all day, or does she just rest and enjoy the clouds. Or, is she sitting on my shoulders? Many say that she is looking out for us – that, I believe. Another question that I have is – can men become angels? Well that may be too much for God to answer, but I bet He has an answer.

Today, I received an e-mail from an attorney in Cleveland stating that he wanted to hear about how Virginia died in the major hospital, and he asked if an autopsy had been performed. He also asked if any lawyer had investigated the case. At first I wanted to jump on this opportunity and send all of the information regarding what we know about her death to him, but as I was putting it all together and inserting information, my computer screen suddenly went blank, and I lost all contact with the attorney. His e-mail disappeared; my response disappeared, and I could not bring any of it up. I sat back for a few minutes and thought about what had just happened. I murmured out loud, "Dinny, did you do that? Don't you want me to proceed with this?" Suddenly out of nowhere, the lawyer's e-mail appeared on the screen of my computer. As I went to answer it, it again vanished. This really happened; I did not make it up.

So, Virginia, your wonderful name will never be subjected to any adverse scrutiny. You will remain in our hearts as a living, breathing tribute to our sixty years together as man and wife. Enjoy your mom, your dad, your sisters and brothers, my mom and dad, and your everlasting life. Your angel wings are well earned. Eventually our paths will cross again, and when it does, what a wonderful thing that will be. Your exit from our home has left me with a broken heart. I live for the day when you stand at my side again, and we feel that warm embrace of our hearts as they meet. My life has been empty since you left. In death, I will be born again, as we share a place in heaven. God does, in fact, work in strange ways, but love is always in his heart. If and when I get to heaven, you, Dinny, will have a lot to do with it; of that I am certain.

Tomorrow, I will be working on my boat to get it ready to run fishing charters. I will have to do it by myself this time as Dinny won't be there to help. She always waxed the hull for me and did the things that needed to be done without a reminder from me. She created a "homey" feeling for that boat, and made up the bed and galley where she stocked the refrigerator, which she often scrubbed. Boy, how I miss her being there! She enjoyed the boat as much as I do. It was an annual ritual. When we had the big "Miss Majestic," the 72 feet long head boat, she used to wax the whole damn hull all by herself. How she did it, I do not know, but she did and asked for no help. That was her job, and she was so proud when she finished. This is the first spring that she will not be there to help and to share the love of putting the boat in the water. She loved to fish, and the lake was her therapy, for she was always happy and laughing when we took a fishing trip out. At one point in our marriage, Dinny used to set lines as was a top notch first mate. She enjoyed the fishing, but it was a good excuse to be with me, and that is what made our marriage work – we enjoyed each other.

Again, I ask my questions –

What will she look like?

Will I know her?

I still have her ring on; will we still be married?

Why is it so hard for me to accept the fact that she is in heaven and safe without pain?

I do not know; I can't answer that … but as I write this book, I hope to learn the answer. Some day …

At Nine Months …

It is May 20th, and my fishing season has started. The fishing, so far, has been great! I miss Virginia on the boat with me because she always made the customers happy. Her smile and her good nature made happy ventures. She loved to perch fish, and at times gave me a run for my money in catching those fish. She also enjoyed walleye fishing and did a great job pulling walleye. Dinny became good at setting lines for trawling, because she just loved being with me, and I enjoyed her company. No matter what we did, we did it together. That was the secret of our sixty years of marriage. We played together; we worked together, and we cried together. We loved each other deeply, and our life together was fun. Virginia was a beautiful woman, both inside and out. From our two children we had Lisa, Joney, Christy, and Nicole, and because of them, we had our great grandchildren – Ashley and Gary. Through her fifteen years of physically suffering, Dinny still laughed, smiled, and put up a good front.

Again, when she went to the last hospital, she warned me that she was not coming home, but I dismissed it. After her surgery, Virginia repeated that she was not coming home, and I became alarmed and told her that she was going to be okay. Well, as it turned out, she was right. She came back to Lorain, but to a grave. To this day, I cannot accept her death, and that is the reason that I write this book. Why did I choose the title as a good title for the book? Why? We all agreed on *Good Grief*, after some of the shock dissipated. We agreed that her death was better now than in years to become a vegetable, and to die a slow death in a home somewhere. No matter how our family mulled it over in our minds, it was her time to go. God had decided that she suffered enough. I think that she was trying to tell me that, but I did not listen to her. I only hope and pray that she is with her siblings and parents, because I know that she is happy, and that is all I care about. I will always love you, Dinny, and tell God thanks from me for letting me have you for all of these years.

You made my life a joyful one. Good night, Dinny, until we meet again. As I write this, you could float a battleship in my tears, but it will not sink my love for you.

Yours forever,

Bob XXX

Today is May 26th, Memorial Day, 2008. Holidays always seem to bring out the sad reality that loved ones are gone. But today is the day to remember the fallen soldiers who have given their lives so that we can remain free - free to worship, free to travel, free to vote, and free to write this book. Virginia has been gone now for almost nine months. I still find myself yelling, "Dinny where is this or that?" She spoiled me badly, and I am the kind of person who needs love and to be loved. She watched over me like a "mother hen," and I loved it! Many of you who have lost a loved one can relate to that; I'm sure. I still have not sorted out the question about heaven and spirits. It becomes more complicated every day. Some people say that the Bible tells us that we cannot contact a spirit. But then, of course, when someone like Sylvia Brown talks to a person and brings fine details to the grieving, others say that she is talking to the devil. If it is so, I would say that it is very nice of the devil to bring hope and love to the grieving. I want so much to contact my wife and to reaffirm my love to her now more than ever. Cannot the naysayer realize the joy and happiness it brings when a spirit brings the afterworld to one's home and allows the griever to enjoy a few, brief moments of contact with one's departed loved ones? From what I have been told by others, they have experienced out-of-world contact many times and in many different ways, but still things that cannot be explained are brushed aside by skeptics. If we can talk to God, we can talk to our loved ones. He would want that contact of love. As I continue with this book, I want to get more first-hand accounts of these contacts to see how real they are. The one I had in the bath tub was real, that's for sure. That sweater flew off that hanger over my head and landed on my chest. The first thing that I did was to thank God for letting her do that.

Since I started to write this book, I have asked the same old questions over and over. The big question I ask now is, "Where do we go from here?" I am sure that we all have, at one time or another, asked this question. The fact is that no matter how one looks at it, that is one event in life that we all have to face. When we die, do we live on in heaven, or do we end our days in a place called hell. I'm certain that many of us know the answer to that question. If one's life has been one of greed and not caring for others, Judgment Day will be a long and painful experience. On the other hand, one does not have to be a Mother Teresa to enter heaven. Good will and love are two good starts.

I know that sometimes when life closes in, there is a feeling that there is nowhere to go and no place to hide. I almost feel as though it is time to leave this world and to join those who have passed on years ago. When Dinny died, I went home, lay down, and begged the Lord to get me up there with her. I told Him, "Lord, I don't care how you do it, but please get me up there with her." I absolutely had no fear whatever. I just wanted to be near her. There is an old saying, "There is nothing more certain than death and taxes." Mark Twain also had another interesting observation about death, "You take heaven; I'd rather go to Bermuda." Wood Allen, on the same topic, once said, "It's not that I am afraid to die, I just don't want to be there when it happens." Another thought is "One might better sail the Atlantic in a paper boat than to get to heaven on good works."

A skeptic would ask, "How many have ever been to heaven and returned?" Interestingly enough, the Bible tells us that three people have done so – Paul, John and Jesus. So it is, without a doubt, a magnificent place, and our new bodies will be beyond comprehension. Our minds will have super powers which are beyond our wildest dreams.

Many of us on earth believe that we are now in hell and are being judged. At times, it may seem that this is true, yet this world of ours is a beautiful place, painted in color, with all sorts of beautiful creatures and plants, and our bodies are such wonderful creations.

Spending my life with a woman like Virginia was a gift from heaven, for she made my life a wonderful experience. It was not without pain and sorrow at times, with sickness and health, but it was also filled with the deep and honest love that we shared together. I deeply regret the day that I ever talked her into going to the hospital for the final surgery. I still cannot understand how a person can drown in her own vomit, while in a major metropolitan hospital. Oh sure, she was 80 years old, but she looked 60, and the local doctors gave her a true bill of health for her operation that was a success, but the aftercare failed. God bless you, Honey. I guess the Lord just figured that you suffered enough. Lord, we hope and pray that You hold her in Your heart, and we pray that she is happy and pain free. God bless you, Dinny. We all miss you terribly.

As many know, grief can cause our moods to change in an instant. Without warning, our minds take us back in time to that day that weighs so heavily in our hearts. We try to give our feelings some solace by trying to recall all of the good days and the great times we had together. Sometimes it works – sometimes it does just the opposite, because we can still see their smiles and hear their laughter. At times it makes us mad that he or she was taken from us so unexpectedly. I know that in my case, I get to that point, and I shout out loud, "Why, why, why did You take her now?" She was on her way back to a normal way of life, free from pain. At least that is what we thought. Maybe God had seen enough of her suffering and decided to make a better life for her. I hope and pray that I am right. We were only thinking about ourselves and did not want to let her go. She made our lives so happy that we failed to see the extent of her pain. I talk to her every night and every morning to make certain that she hears from me.

When I was looking for a title for this book, I thought of grief right away, and at that time, I was a wreck! I cried myself to sleep every night, and awakened crying every morning. My daughter told me to get some pills to dull the pain, but then a thought came to me. I'm supposed to cry. I'm supposed to grieve. That is part of life, yet it turned into *Good Grief*, and that is what I did. Now I concentrate on what a beautiful woman she was, and all of the great times we had together. I love her smile, her voice, her actions, and her loving ways. There are still times that I cry, but it's grief, good grief in remembering such a wonderful person and thanking the Lord for letting me have her for all of these years. If a person does not try to handle his/her grief, it can drive him/her made, and the loved one does not want that, I'm sure. Now I wonder if she can see or hear me. I should not be crying and carrying on and make her feel badly. It must be agonizing enough to endure the act of dying by drowning in one's own vomit.

Experts say that heaven is beyond our comprehension – beautiful beyond words. There, there is no more pain or sorrow, no more hate or jealousy, and it tests our imagination to even think that this can be possible. As I have said previously, some claim that we are in hell now, and we are being tested for everlasting life in heaven. I have no doubts about Dinny's destination. She is up there and has earned her wings. But in my case, I've been busy here on earth, making a life for my family. I have been a good husband and a good father but have done very little for others. The thing that bothers me now is, at 82 years old, do I start to earn my ticket to heaven, or does my love and devotion to family count enough to get me there? I do ask for His forgiveness, and have asked Him repeatedly to watch over my wife, my family, and friends.

I have been blessed all of my life with great parents, great kids, and a wonderful wife. The Lord got me through World War II, practically unscathed, and gave me an angel to live with for all of these years – talk about lucky! As Lou Gehrig once said, "I am the luckiest guy on this earth," and I do feel that way. I have lots of friends, and those who haven't taken the time to know me, hate me, and that's sad, because I basically love people.

Virginia and I loved the lake, and we spent as much time as we could there. We became friends with lots of boaters at the Spitzer's Marina here in Lorain. When Virginia passed away, the boaters were there for me and shared my loss: Bo and Linda, Claudia and Rick, Bill and Cathy, Kenny, Tommy, Frank, Gary and his wife, Popey, Jim, Jim, Iman and his wife, Pappy and Joe. There were hundreds more who met Virginia on the *Miss Majestic* and fell in love with her. Chuck and Della Nitola were very close friends with whom Virginia and I fell in love. It is such a good feeling to recall all of one's friends.

It is now June 5, 2008, and I am getting a self-help course in cooking, washing, and cleaning the house. I have to admit that I am not good at any one of those things. I cannot imagine how to take care of kids on top of all of this. I have a newly found appreciation on being a woman and having to do all of that – not an easy job. A few days I became hungry and could not figure out what to eat. I searched through the kitchen, but all of the meals that I came up with were too much work. I needed something easy to make, then I spotted a box of Bisquick, a pancake mix. Hell, I thought to myself, that's not hard to make. Virginia used to turn those pancakes out in a minute flat. Well I grabbed the box, sat down, and read the instructions. I got the fry pan, buttermilk, eggs, and mixed up the batter. I wanted to make a little bit, but it was too thin, so I added some more of the Bisquick, but then it was too thick, so I added some milk. Now I had enough to feed the hungry in Africa. I scooped up the batter and poured it into the fry pan, and did what the instructions read, "to wait until it starts to bubble, then turn it over. I did, and now I have a pile of crap in the pan. I scraped it up and threw it away and started all over again. I have lots of this stuff left in the bowl for practice. The next time I was lucky. It flipped over great, and in a few minutes I had a beautiful pancake. I was so proud of myself that I got out my camera and took a picture of it. I then took a picture of the empty plate after I ate the pancake. Why? I don't know. I have no one but me to whom to show it off.

Boy, how fast life changes when a person has had a wonderful woman to care for you for six decades. I have never been alone at all in my life. Now, for as old as I am and when I need someone to be with, I'm all alone! I talk to Dinny all of the time – in the car, or in the house. I feel like I let her down in the hospital when she said, "I'm not coming home." I ignored her and let it pass over my head. When this happens, a person feels like no one else has every experienced it. The first words out of our mouths is the standard, "Why me?" It is as though I am the only one to suffer like this. For months you try to convince yourself that this did not happen, and that you will wake up the next day, and your loved one will be right at your side. As time elapses, the reality becomes apparent – she's gone. Then the new process starts, and you all know what I mean. Where is she? How is she? The questions keep coming. If you are fortunate enough to have the religious faith that convinces you, then you don't need to ask these questions. God bless you. It is not that I do not believe, it's just that after sixty years with someone whom you love so deeply, you forget about the religious factor and begin to worry about her. Many of us have had that aspect of life pounded into our heads that death is a part of life, so accept it – not too easy to do. I'm sorry if I repeat myself in this book and rave about Virginia, but she was truly a beautiful woman with a heart of gold. That reminds me, I have to send a donation to the St Jude Shriner's Hospital and to the St. Labre Indian School in Montana. Virginia never failed to send them money, when I had to practically fight with her to buy herself something. She was always buying for others.

These are the many things I miss about Virginia, but the thing I miss most is having her near and hugging her. She was always there with outstretched arms. Now she has the wings, and I hope and pray that she is happy and pain free. I look forward to the day when we meet again. Thanks, Dinny for a wonderful life together.

Today is Father's Day. I went out to Virginia's grave and talked with her today. I have written a poem about her death and dedicated it to her. I have included it here at the end of this section of the book. I have been running charters about three times a week, and it helps me to get my mind off of her passing. Yet, she was so much of a part of my life that everywhere I look, I am reminded of her. She was on the boat a lot, and she enjoyed fishing immensely. If she was not on the boat, she always met it when I came in to port. I now invariably look for her on the deck when I return. She always had something for me, whether it was a can of pop, a new shirt, or a pair of swimming trunks.

This week, I took Dinny's two surviving sisters out to lunch. One is 86 years old; the other is 84. They were both very close to Dinny, even though they came from a large family and had a tough life growing up. That's what bothers me so much. My wife, Virginia, came through the operation fine, but someone let her down when she needed him or her most. She should be with me right now. After talking with other people, I am finding out that this sort of thing happens more than we think. I won't dwell on that too much because it upsets me thoroughly.

The weather here has been beautiful this past week with a few rain storms, but nothing too bad. The Midwest of our country has been hit badly. I think of those poor people, and then I realize how lucky I am. Many of those people have lost everything – home and possessions as well as some, if not all of their family members. As bad as things are for us personally, there is always someone else worse off. It's funny, sometimes, as I sit here in the house, I try to talk with my wife. I challenge her to show me a sign. I even concentrate really hard to try to emulate Sylvia Brown. How come we can't do that -- to contact the spirit world. I may be wrong, but I do believe in her and John Edwards.

I think that it would be nearly impossible to fake that sort of thing. It is very interesting that Virginia used to like to watch them both.

I changed the oil in the boat today. The weather cooled off a little, so I took advantage of it. I have a charter coming up in two days for fishing for walleye. Let's see, in about twelve days, I will be eighty-two years old, with my birthday on the 27th of June, and it would have been our 61st wedding anniversary. No matter how I try, this book is going to be about her and me. It was a love story, and it still is.

After More Than A Year ...

It has been a year and seven months since Virginia died, and my life has changed dramatically. I no longer look forward to coming home, because the house has become an empty shell. The beautiful smell of great meals cooking on the stove or in the oven has disappeared. Her warm greeting and happy smile is gone. I still have trouble understanding why such a wonderful person like she had to have such a painful life and die such a torturous death. I have to admit, God has tried to help me to understand. All of a sudden, people from Jehovah's Witness begin to visit our home. I sit and open my heart to them. I seem to watch religious programs on the television more than I ever did. I have even opened the Bible and tried to understand what it means. The daughter of the captain of the destroyer I was on during World War II called me to advise that the admiral had died on March 2, 2009. We sat and talked on the phone for an hour about life and death. She shocked me with a statement about the admiral. He did not believe in God, nor did he believe in heaven. He was such a highly intelligent man, yet he was unsure of life's outcome. In a way, I was sad that he turned out to be a nonbeliever. Here I am, a man who feels sorry for his belief system, when I, myself, am looking for so many answers. As I have said before in this book, all one has to do is to look around, and God's work is obvious. Our world is one giant jigsaw puzzle with all its parts fitting nicely into place.

I feel so all alone now. Our years together passed like a blink of an eye. My daughter and I keep looking for signs – a penny here, a penny there – just something to hold on to. When we find a penny now, it makes us feel so good – as if Virginia has placed that penny into our hands. My son, Bob, and daughter, Carol, are both convinced that their mom is okay. The location and timing of these pennies make it hard not to believe that only she could have put them there. So pennies from heaven have come into our hearts. I still worry about how Virginia is, and where she is, but I know in my heart of hearts that she is with God and her family, yet I torture myself with the thought that maybe she is not where I wish her to be. I am a worrier by nature, and have been all of my life. I can't seem to relax and to let the world go by. I thought I had all of this stuff sorted out, but when Dinny died, it all hit me right to my core. I still ask myself, how in the hell does a person drown in one's own vomit in a major hospital, which consistently brags about being the best? I just don't understand how that hospital such remarkable achievements over the years, yet slips up on aftercare of a patient. This question will haunt our hearts and minds forever. How did this happen? So far, we have no answers.

How does one make a marriage last for sixty years or more? My advice is that husbands should make their wives their buddies. Married couples should spend time together and be considerate of each other's feelings, as well as they should hug and kiss each other and let one another know that they care. I'm finding out just how much work it is to take care of a home, washing, cooking, and doing it all by myself. This is one hell of a lot of work, and all I have to do is to take care of me. What if I had kids to tend? Boy, a woman's work is not for me. It's never done! My work was from 8:00 a.m. to 3:30 p.m. – that's a lot better deal!

The one thing that is so hard for me is the empty feeling of loneliness. A person can only watch television for so long before I get really bored. The Internet and this computer have helped me to get through this chapter of my life. A forum to talk to other people has been a big help. I have tried to be a person to lift others up with jokes and laughter. I find it hard sometimes to pursue this course of action, but in life, I always tried to keep a smile on my face and a joke or two on my lips. I used to sing to Virginia, "Have I Told You Lately That I Love You," and it always put a smile on her face.

My only advice to a young couple is, "Don't be so serious. Laugh and laugh often, but be responsible and true to each other." Virginia was always there for me, and she never let me down. I still and will always love her with all my heart. God bless you, Dinny.

Love,

Bob

DINNY!!

Her name is Virginia, my Buddy, my pal,
She is now with her mother, her mom's name is Sal,
Her brothers, her sisters, her Dad, and a dog named Pal.
This beautiful lady that I've loved all these years
Has brought me to losing these unblemished years
Now I have nothing but memories, she gone from this earth.
The Old Lord said, Dinny, you've suffered enough
Come join me in heaven with your wings here await
You're welcome to come in. We opened the gate.
Your loved ones will miss you and you'll miss them too
But soon they will join you and what a joy that will be
What a heavenly party that we will all be there to see.
So, Dinny, we all love you, your son, your daughter and me
We'll see you in heaven if the Old Lord says it's okay to be.
Love, Bob

My Beautiful Virginia

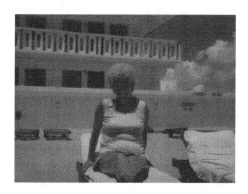

Happy With Her Catches!

My Pal

Our Fishing Charter's First Anniversary

A Family Thanksgiving Feast

FORUM'S STORIES

Living here on this earth, nothing is more important than believing in our soul and having faith in the hereafter. Life without hope of everlasting life, is a life wasted. I always felt that life here on earth is too complex to ignore how and why we are here. My wife, Virginia, and I often discussed this subject, and I felt that as long as you believed in God and His son, Jesus, your chances of your spirit living on were much better. In other words, it was and is still my contention that even though you didn't go to church, or many times didn't live up to the 10 Commandments, as long as you tried to live a clean life and believed in God, you are to be forgiven. There is really no reason for our existence, if there is no hereafter. Our own bodies are a living testament of the creation of heaven and earth. The amazing functions of our minds that is our flesh and blood that can move our arms, turn our heads, move our legs, and look out at this world with our eyes, is proof of God's wonderful creations. So many times, I have looked at my hands and moved my fingers and thought to myself, "Wow, isn't that something!" It has been said that we are using only one thousandth of our brain that the capacity of our brain is much higher than we think. Some people may say lots of us don't use our brains at all. But how can we ignore this wonderful machine that the Lord has built for us? We smoke, we drink, and abuse our bodies and even have tattoos placed on our skin, hiding this cover that God has given us. As you grow older, you tend to look at these things and wonder why we do that to our bodies. We also suddenly look to God for relief of pain as arthritis and old age creep up on us. Right at this point of my life I have a serious back problem and am scheduled for an operation. My wife will not be there with me this time, as she has been in the past, but I know her spirit will be with me. In the early years of marriage, you have no idea what love is until you grow old together. Then you realize what life is all about. Companionship --having someone you love close to you when you need her or him. When that person dies, your life turns upside down. As I said earlier in this book – suddenly nothing seems to matter, and you suffer the anguish of loneliness that tears your heart out. There is nothing else like it. I feel the sorrow that must be felt by mothers and fathers of soldiers killed in action overseas. The pain inside is something you never see. But I do believe God has a special place in His heart for these young men and women. God bless them. We may never know the answers to these after death questions, until death takes our bodies to the grave and our spirits are taken before our maker. That's enough of my preaching, so let's get on with some words from people who have a better understanding about this than I do.

The following pages are some of the answers that I received from folks whom I asked questions about heaven and life after death. Will I see my wife again, etc. Before my wife's death, I was so sure about all of this, yet now after she is gone, I grieve for her so much that it eats into my faith. Before she died, I constantly reminded her of God's love and assured her that there was everlasting life. I recall telling her, "All you have to do is to look around you and see God's work. There would be no use at all for us being here, if this was the end." But once death comes to a family, you seek out support for your beliefs. In any event, here are some answers. The readers can sort them out and see how many people are lost in this sea of uncertainty. Yet we must believe in God and heaven.

FORUM - I am *praying for you that you find your answer in the Bible so that is the only place that has the truth. God wants us to know Him and He tells us who He is and who we are in the Bible. We have a book from God and we need to see what He has to say to us. If you have any questions, please ... ask us and we will try to answer you.*

BOB – I hope to get more people involved and get their answers to my questions as I sit here typing this. I cannot believe that I am writing a book on religion. God, I think you picked the wrong guy for this job. What I know about religion, and the hereafter, can be put in the eye of a needle. But He gave me this job, so I'll just keep typing away to see where it goes. Today is April 1, 2008, and I put my boat in the water, and this is the first time I did it without my Dinny. She was always there and had her camera to take pictures. When I opened the cabin door, I found her sweatshirt that I had made for her. It was a nice blue hooded Sweatshirt with "First Mate – Virginia" printed on the front and big letters on the back – "Majestic Fishing Charters." I folded it up and laid it on the bed so that it will be there for her, if she needs it.

After I came home from the boat, I went to Pete's Restaurant, here in

Lorain. Pete's wife came over to my table and said hello. I met her before, and of times told her of my struggle with the grief of my wife dying. We talked a lot about her death and about death in general and the hereafter. I was not aware of the fact that she could contact the spirits. I put a little ring of Virginia's on my left pinky finger. I call it my Angel's ring. She asked to hold the ring in her fingers and continuously moved it in her fingers. She came up with some answers that in no way she could have guessed them. She spoke of things about our life together, and things about our home. Her explanation regarding spirits and how they look made sense to me. She said, "Spirits can and do transform themselves into the visions a person wants to see, so yes, you will see your wife again, and she will appear just as you remember her. This I like as she was beautiful woman. But then I asked if I can kiss and hug her. She said, "God loves you, and He loves her. You both will be happy in heaven." Then she said, in effect, don't push your luck, stick with the facts and promote God's love. The rest of these questions will be answered in time. I sent a letter to a church in Chicago that has a website. They claim to answer the questions that I have. I have not read it yet, but hope that I can get some insight into this very private hereafter heaven I hear so much about. I will add their comments, if they approve of my using their information.

FORUM – *I am sorry for the loss of your wife of 60 years. I realize also that knowing where she is and whether you will be reunited after death is important to you. God's Word give those who have put their faith in Jesus Christ the hope of eternal life after this earthly life and reunited with those who have also put their faith in Christ. We will know and be known by family and friends. No more sorrow, tears or heartache. The scriptures are full of the promises of God's hope and future life. We can have that tope today when we look to the life, death, and Resurrection of Christ, when we, by faith, put our trust in Him.*

I pray you will have access to a Bible and a follower of Christ, a Christian, in your community who can help you discover God's purpose for the remainder of your life here and into eternity.

BOB – Thank you very much for taking time out of your busy schedule to answer my mail. I would love to sit down and talk with you sometime when you are free for a few minutes. I believe in Jesus and His Father, but God gave me an open mind and an inquisitive nature. He wants me to be that way. Then why can't I question where my wife is and how she is? The real question I always hear is, "Who made God." Of course, all you have to do to realize God is here is to look around you at the trees, the sky, the birds, our hands, our feet, our eyes. We were created by our Maker. Why can't we know "The truth and whole truth and nothing but the truth, so help me God." Why is it such a secret? The one whom I loved most of all on earth is dead and buried. Why shouldn't I seek more information? I understand where you will go with this. We do not have the right to question our faith. We are to follow our belief in the Lord and obey the Ten Commandments. I try to do that, but I still worry about that wonderful lady with whom I shared my life. I can't help it. God bless you, sir, and thanks again for your time. God and I have sailed together for years. I have a guardian angel on my shoulder, and it is my wife, if only she could talk to me.

FORUM – *I think you have every right to ask where your wife is. I'm sorry if my previous e-mail gave you the idea that this would not be a question you should ask.*

You say you believe in Jesus and His Father. This must have come from growing up around a Christian influence. If your wife also had faith in Jesus, then she is saved. You will see each other in Heaven and know each other. You might read Romans 5:1-11 from the New Testament scriptures. This is a great passage of scripture for all who look to Christ.

You might also read Jeremiah 29:11-14 from the Old Testament. Great promise of God that if we will seek Him we can know the truth, the whole truth.

Hope this helps you.

BOB – Thanks. That brings a tear to my eyes – Oh my God, how I miss that girl! She came from a strong Catholic family, and although I was a Protestant, we never let that come between us. She had our house and yard full of angels. She lived her life for others, and she spoiled me rotten. I thank you so much for your mail. It's funny, in a way, I used to preach to her about God and teller her if there is nothing after life on earth, then there is no us to even being here. All you have to do is to look around you to see God's work. This didn't just happen. There is too much planning. All of the parts of the puzzle work. Again, God bless you for your message.

FORUM – *It sounds like you both had the same Christian values growing up. Whether she was Catholic and you were Protestant is not a problem with God. Both religions draw their understanding and teachings from God's Word, the Holy Bible.*

What is important is the relationship with God through Jesus Christ, not the religion you were under.

There are lots of Catholics and Protestants going to Heaven together.

Blessings,

FORUM – *Dear Navy,*

I am so sorry to hear of your loss and am praying that you find peace, for your sake and your wonderful wife's Virginia. She cannot return to you. I encourage you to read in 2 Sam 12 when David's son was dying.

2 Samuel 12:23 KJV But now he is dead, wherefore should I fast? Can I bring him back again? I shall go to him, but he shall not return to me.

We cannot bring our loved ones back in spirit or otherwise as this is not wise. As then we can invoke evil spirits instead of the one that we loved, who mimic our loved ones and deceive us. And it is not a good idea to invoke the spirits of those who have died, see 1 Samuel 28:11.

I encourage you to read the Bible for your answers to your questions. They can all be found there.

When I found out about some of them I wrote a poem I would like to share with you that may help you.

"To Catch a Glimpse"

Beyond our dimension of time and space, abides our God in an awesome place. He's not behind a comet, or on mars, you can't seek Him out among the stars. Yet his spirit sits on the circle of our earth, keeping track of each new birth.

He rides the clouds like chariots and walks upon the wings of the wind, yet He still has time to be my best friend. He guides me through each day, carries me when I lose my way.

I can almost see His face, His glory so bright, shining throughout the place. O, to be with Him forever more. Want your dreams to all come true? Can't imagine what He has in store for you?

Can you imagine happy ever after? Never tears, only laughter. Never ever be lonely again. Never having to worry about sin. Imagine your mansion fifteen acres square, all your acquaintances gathered there.

We won't need a telephone with an added dimension we could be in another place in the blink of an eye. Imagine the distances we could cross just to say, "HI!" Children dancing in a golden square, true love and brotherhood everywhere. Never a worry, woe, or care. It all can be found nowhere but there.

The garden of God will be totally cool, swimming in a crystal clear pool. Fruit on every single tree, never getting stung by a bee. Climbing mountains to the top, never feeling the cold. Never again aging or growing old.

Imagine earth all redone, room enough for everyone! The Milky Way our playground, Joyful singing the only sound, music never heard in this realm. I'll carry a parrot on each arm, and walk with a lion by my side. Why would one want to hide from God?

The plans He has for me are beyond my wildest dreams, surpassing my husband's craziest schemes. We could plant the universe and the blossoms will never face away. Singing His praises for always. Before we call He will answer. While we are yet speaking He will hear. Never again feeling fear.

I have but a glimpse of what lies beyond this earthly sphere. But I can hear His voice as He walks upon the wings of the wind. Have you heard Jesus call your name? If you answer, your life will never be the same!

May God bless and keep you in the palm of His hand,

FORUM – *I have zero doubt that you will know your wife and she will know you, when you meet in Heaven. I also have o reluctance in saying that, if your desire is to hug her and kiss her, then that is exactly what you will do.*

The scripture in Matt 22:30 is a response that Jesus gave to someone who was asking about a woman who had been married so seven different brothers. They wanted to know which one's wife she would be when she got to heaven.

I have a son who has preceded me in going to heaven. When I get to heaven, he will be no less my son that he was while we were both here on earth. But … I will no longer have the parental position, and responsibility, for him that I had while he was here on earth.

Jesus said they would not "marry" or "be given in marriage" at the resurrection (of our BODIES) from the dead. They were asking Him, specifically about the resurrection.

The spirits of our departed loved ones are already there (in Heaven), providing they had previously accepted the sacrifice that Jesus made for them on The Cross. Just as our new, resurrected bodies will not marry, or be given in marriage, neither will my resurrected body give birth again.

The question was presented to Jesus with an air of jealousy (a human emotion), asking which brother was going to claim her as HIS wife, etc. Actually it was presented in an attempt to trip Him up, but it didn't work.

This is the beauty of Heaven … There will be no jealousy there, because EVERYONE will be the same. There will be no humans in positions of hierarchy. There will be no leaders. A husband will no longer be the "head," or authority over his wife/family. We will have no need of marriage licenses or birth certificates, in order to proe our rights and atttachments to other people. Here on earth we try to claim equality for all, but when we get to Heaven that dream will finally be true.

The ONLY Head or authority in Heaven, will be the Triune God – Father, Son, and Holy Ghost.

There will be no jealousy. If everyone is equal there is no purpose to it. No competition of any kind. No titles. No reason for "legal," earthly titles and attachments.

There will be nothing but LOVE…pure love, for and by everyone present. Our very being will be engulfed by LOVE, because God, Himself "IS" LOVE. You won't be looking at your wife with any feelings of possessiveness as if you have a claim to stake, to keep her for yourself. No one can/will take her from you. She will be loved by you and by everyone else … equally. Just as you will be loved by her, and everyone else who is there … equally. LOVE is the number one requirement for being there! EVERYONE will love EVERYONE, equally!

How awesome does that sound?

Navy, I hope I haven't confused you more. I wish I had more time, but right now I don't. I hope this will ease your mind a bit, and if I can help you in the future, PLEASE let me know.

BOB – Okay, here are some of my questions. First of all before I ask them, I want you to know that I ask these questions only because I don't know the answers. Not that I want to put you down in any way, I don't think anyone, but God, knows the answers. And when I read his words, I cannot understand them. So far, I have different answers for my other questions from other pastors, priests, and rabbis. First of all, where is heaven?

FORUM – *Heaven is a spiritual place; it's not in a physical dimension.*

BOB – What will we look like in heaven?

FORUM – *When Jesus returned to the apostles after He rose from the dead, He was in a new transfigured body. He appeared the same, yet He could walk through walls somehow. We all get new bodies when we pass on.*

BOB – If we are spirits in the after world, then why did God promise us everlasting life?

FORUM – *We get everlasting life in our spirit bodies. Our physical body can't hold up forever.*

BOB – A spirit is not life, or am I wrong?

FORUM – *It's a continuation of our life. We will see those we knew before. We will all know each other.*

BOB – What quality of life does a spirit have?

FORUM – *The best. No pain, no suffering. We live together in joy and love.*

BOB – If my wife is now a spirit, can I hug her, kiss her, or doesn't that happen?

FORUM – *I think so, but you will have many others there whom you will wish to see again, as well.*

BOB – Will she still be my wife? I am asking the questions that everyone else is afraid to ask?

FORUM – *We aren't married in heaven as we are on earth. It's more like we are married/united/joined to everyone in heaven. We don't lose anything, we gain everything.*

BOB – What will be so great about heaven that we will all enjoy it. Does the Bible explain this?

FORUM – *Here are a couple of Bible commentaries on heaven. They also give you verses you may wish to read as well.*

Heaven

A word that expresses several distinct concepts in the Bible:
1. *As used in a physical sense, heaven is the expanse over the earth (Gen.1:8). The tower of Babel reached upward to heaven (Gen. 11:4). God is the possessor of heaven (Gen. 14:19). Heaven is the location of the stars (Gen. 1:14; 26:4) as well as the source of dew (Gen. 27:28).*
2. *Heaven is also the dwelling place of God (Gen. 28:17; Rev. 12:7-8). It is the source of the new Jerusalem (Rev. 21:2, 10). Because of the work of Christ on the Cross, heaven is, in part, present with believers on earth as they obey God's commands (John 14:2, 23).*
3. *The word heaven is also used as a substitute for the name of God (Luke 15:18,21; John 3:27). The kingdom of God and the kingdom of heaven are often spoken of interchangeably (Matt. 4:17; Mark 1:15).*
4. *At the end of time a new heaven will be created to surround the new earth. This new heaven will be the place of God's perfect presence (Isa. 65:17; 66:22; Rev. 21:1). Then there will be a literal fulfillment of heaven on earth.*

(from Nelson's Illustrated Bible Dictionary, Copyright 1986, Thomas Nelson Publishers)

Heaven

From "heaved up;" so "the heights" (Ps 148:1). The Greek <u>ouranos</u> and the Hebrew <u>shamayim</u>, are similarly derived. It is used of the surrounding air wherein "the fowls of heaven" fly (Gen 1:26), compare (Gen. 1:20); from whence the rain and hail fall (Deut. 11:11). "I will make your heaven as iron, "i.e., your sky hard and yielding no rain (Lev. 26:19). "The four quarters of heaven" (Jer. 49:36) and "the circuit of heaven" (Job 22:14) refer to the atmospheric heaven. By metaphor it is represented as a building with foundations and pillars (2 Sam. 22:8; Job 26:11), with an entrance gate (Gen. 28:17) and windows opened to pour down rain (Gen. 7:11, compare 2 Kings 7:2; Mal 3:10). Job 37:18, "spread out the sky ... strong ... as a molten rain.

FORUM – *There is hope. That is why Jesus came to earth. He died in our place – He took on our sin so that we can one day live with Him. What part of that do you not like?*

BOB – There are no angels ---

FORUM – *Nowhere did I say there are no angels. I said that we are not to worship them. Only God is to be worshipped.*

BOB – There is no way for the spirits to contact us.

FORUM – *I showed you from the Bible that we are not to contact the dead. Which part of God's Word do you want to throw out?*

BOB – It seems like you put more faith in the devil than you do in the Lord.

FORUM – *I give you God's Word, and you say it is from the devil? (Rom. 10:17) So then faith comes by hearing and hearing by the Word of God.*

BOB – Hey when you're dead, you're dead. No hope, just gloom. Someday maybe you will be saved, maybe.

FORUM - *Please point me to the post where I said that?*

BOB – Wait until you have been married for sixty years, and you lose your loved one. You place a lot of trust in the devil and blame him for everything you don't understand.

FORUM – *I understand God's Word. Why do you want to throw it out?*

BOB – I love our Lord, and He loves me. I know that.

FORUM – *Okay, then show me Bible verses that say that. (I'm not saying it isn't true, but I want you to go to the Bible and show me).*

BOB – And, I also know if it wasn't my wife who contacted me, then it was God, Himself, because I felt the love in the messages.

FORUM – *I gave you verses from the Bible that say the opposite.*

BOB – The more I read of this, the more confused I get. If and when I get to heaven, if I do … the information that I am getting doesn't seem to paint a fun place. As a spirit, my wife won't be able to kiss me. I can't hug her. We are no longer married. How joyous will that be?

FORUM – *John 20:26 – 29 KJV – And after eight days again his disciples were within, and Thomas with them: then came Jesus, the doors being shut, and stood in the midst, and said, Peace be unto you. (27) Then saith he to Thomas, Reach higher thy finger, and behold my hands; and reach higher thy hand, and thrust it into my side: and be not faithless, but believing. (28) And Thomas answered and said unto him, My Lord and my God. (29) Jesus saith unto him, Thomas, because thou has seen me, thou has believed: blessed are they that have not seen and yet have believed.*

BOB – But I'm not convinced about death and what happens. She has contact me three or four times now, so she must be okay, but I still worry about her. She's all I had, and I still love her.

FORUM – *I truly believe that her spirit will never leave you as long as you need her. She IS at peace. There is no pain, but I think she will be with you until you can move on without her, and have some peace, and then she will be there less and less until you are both together again.*

FORUM – *Dear Sir,*

My husband passed a few years ago, so I can relate to your grief and loneliness. I just wanted to offer you a word of caution. Not all of the answers that you will get on a forum will be accurate, according to the Bible. I have already read some of the responses given to your post, that I disagree with 110%. The Bible just does not support what some people say. Many just give their own personal opinion, or what they may have been taught themselves. Please do not misunderstand, I am not claiming to have all of the answers, but I would never answer such serious questions as yours, unless I felt certain, in my heart, that what I am telling you is truth! Bible truth! My suggestion is that you should find someone ... a friend, a pastor ... someone that you have trust and confidence in ... someone who will give you the answers based on the Bible ALONE and not their opinion. Sadly to say ... many people just spout off answers based on thought, prayer or study whatsoever. Like the person telling you that Heaven is not a real (physical) place, but a spiritual place. Well, Navy, the Bible gives the actual measurements of Heaven and even tells – in great detail – about the materials that it will be made out of. Does that not sound "real" to you? I don't want to start arguments with anyone on that forum, by disagreeing with the answers that they have given you; answers that I believe to be either false, or seriously lacking and falling far short of the WHOLE truth, and ... trust me, when you disagree with folks on these forums, they get really upset ... fast. But ... if you think that I can be of help to you in ANY way, please feel free to e-mail me. God Bless you!

BOB – Now see, that's what I mean. John Edwards and Sylvia Brown do talk to the spirits.

FORUM – *Oh, I agree … but the spirits they talk to are not from heaven. At one time Satan was a top angel in heaven, but he wanted to be like God and he was kicked out of heaven. When he left, he took one-third of the angels with him who wanted to follow him. These, are the evil spirits that John and Sylvia speak to. They have been around before the creation of the world and they long to bring man down. This is what the Word of God says about the devil. (1 Peter 5:8-9) Your enemy the devil prowls around like a roaring lion looking for someone to devour.*

BOB – And tons of people believe it.

FORUM – *I know, but that doesn't make it true because tons of people believe it, right?*

BOB – In fact in my new book, I had a girl give me a reading and no way could she come up with the information she had. She even mentioned a bed mattress that is standing on end. Two days ago I removed a mattress from my hide-a-bed and because of my back surgery, I could not take it back upstairs to our spare bedroom, so I leaned it against the wall in the dining room.

FORUM – *Like I said, though, the devil and his followers have been around before mankind and they are very knowledgeable and the last thing they want you to do is to follow God.*

BOB – If the devil can contact us, then why would you think our Lord can't?

FORUM – *God gave us the Torah or what we gentiles call it, the Old Testament. In it, He tells us as who He is and who we are. Lots of stories in there that are there for us to read. In fact, the Torah promised a Savior for the people who are sinners (the Bible says we are all sinners – not hard to figure out, right?) Then one day, God contacted us directly by sending His Son as Savior for all who would believe on Him. This Savior is Jesus Christ. This same Savior was foretold in the Old Testament. When Jesus left this earth to return to heaven, He left us His Holy Spirit to dwell in the believer. We have the Word of God which is how God speaks to us, today. Instead of seeking fallible humans like Silvia and John, wouldn't it be better to read God's Word and let Him speak to you? We have a book from God and not many read it. I suggest starting with the book of John in the New Testament.*

BOB – or our loved ones can't

FORUM – *I gave you verses from the Bible in a previous post that shows they cannot. There is no reason for them to contact us. They have moved on and it is our responsibility to seek God and what He has to say to us which is far more important.*

BOB – Ask any two people to read a section of the Bible and they will come up with two different versions. You can interpret it anyway you want … not to say that you're not right with your version, but it is possible.

FORUM – *You want to give me an example?*

BOB – God put us on this earth to enjoy life, not to become obsessed with religion.

FORUM – *Hey! I agree. Jesus had the following to say. John 10:10 – The thief comes only to steal and kill and destroy; I have come that they may have life, and have it to the full.*

FORUM – *Believing and following Jesus is not being obsessed with religion. Religion never saved anyone. Only Jesus came to save us from the penalty of sin.*

BOB – Many times you hear of people that have killed their families, and they claim God told them to do it. That's just a case of over indulgence with religion.

FORUM – *These same people are not followers of the God of the Bible. Many claim to be God themselves. Many are kooks.*

BOB – You can see what has happened to the Muslim religion. Pray all day, then go out, strap on a bomb, and kill all the people a Muslim can, including his or her own people..

FORUM – *The Muslim religion is one that follows Mohammed – the man was a pedophile. He claimed that what he said just fell from heaven. See, that is how Satan works – very sick stuff.*

BOB – I see God as someone who loves us and doesn't want us to jump through a hoop for him. Live a good, clean life, and God will remember you. My wife was a good example. We had sixty years together with love and compassion.

FORUM – *God didn't make us puppets, but gave all of us a free will to follow Him or not. It is more than living a clean life as if that is left to each of us to* *define. We come up with what is clean and what is not in our own eyes. We need to go to the Bible and allow God to define what is clean and what is not. God has said that we are all sinners and that the penalty for sin is death. The good news, though, is that there is a way out and the way out is believing in Jesus Christ who came to save us from the penalty of sin. Jesus fulfilled scripture and did for us what we could not do for ourselves. He took our punishment by going to the cross and then He died but on the 3rd day, arose from the grave. When we accept Jesus as our Savior, He gives to us His righteousness so that we can one day stand before God blameless. This is what we have on the start page of our*

FORUM- *The Good News: Whether you realize it or not, God wants to establish a personal relationship with you. However, man's sin prevents Him from establishing this relationship. The Bible states in Romans 3:23 " … for all have sinned and fall short of the glory of God." The penalty of man's sin is death, or eternal separation from God, but here is the good news: "For the wages of sin is death, but the gift of God is eternal life in Christ Jesus our Lord," Romans 6:23. How does one receive this gift? According to Romans 10:9, "That if you confess with your mouth, 'Jesus is Lord,' and believe in your heart that God raised Him from the dead, you will be saved." This confession is the beginning of eternal life. This life is a journey of obeying God and living according to His Word (the Bible). To cultivate your relationship with God, you need to spend time reading His Word.*

BOB – God wrote the Ten Commandments.

FORUM – *Is that the only thing you think God has to say to us? The 10 Commandments are in the Bible.*

BOB – Man wrote the Bible ten different times to fit his own sins and beliefs.

FORUM – *Who told you that?*

BOB – When you as a Christian make light of the Catholic religion, that says a lot to me about your faith.

FORUM – *I never mentioned the Catholic religion in any of my posts.*

BOB – I do not want to contact you any more, as you fail to bring joy to my heart, only gloom.

FORUM – *I gave you the Word of God, why do you want to throw it out?*

BOB - I hope that before you die, you have the courage to ask some questions on your own and use the brain that God gave you.

FORUM – *I do and I use it to get into God's Word and seek His wisdom*

BOB – Preach love, not hate of the devil. Please don't answer, as I don't want to debate the issue. You know it all. God bless ya. You have all the answers.

FORUM - *Nowhere did I preach hate. I asked you to get into the Bible and not seek out people like John and Sylvia. I don't have the answers but God does. John and Sylvia make you feel god, but the end is destruction.*

BOB – I have to be very careful on how I respond to your post. First, as you can see, I was happy to hang onto to a piece of my past. My loving wife has contacted me, and if that makes me feel good, why would you want to blame the devil and destroy my happiness.

You have not answered one of my questions from YOUR HEART. You are programmed to verse 10, section 108. Every word you put forth is a quote from the Bible, AND EACH QUESTION THAT YOU DON'T KNOW THE ANSWER TO, YOU BLAME THE DEVIL.

Don't you realize that I have lost the most precious thing in my life, and any contact at all is a Godsend, even if, as you say, the devil sent it. My wife and I did not go to church. We did not brag about it, but we felt the love we had for each other was a gift from God, and we thanked Him every day.

We raised a boy and a girl to be good people and believe in God. My wife was very sick for 15 years and suffered with pain. She was a strict Catholic, yet she married a Protestant and loved angels. She lived a very caring lifestyle, so there is no doubt in my mind that she is an angel. Then I hear there are no angels in heaven, so it seems everything that we want to believe, some say not true. How sad to break someone's heart and look at life as a book. I think the Lord wants more than that. He wants your version through your heart. Have you ever read the poem, "Safely Home" that says it all comes from the heart.

God bless,

FORUM – *Well, Navy, she is contacting you because she is worried about you. I had an experience like that with my father-in-law. He was very close to my hubby (ex.), and he appeared before both of us one night while we were raiding the fridge. We both stood there dumbfounded. We both said, "Did you see what I just saw?" Yes, we both saw.*

My hubby (ex.) was finally able to let go and look forward, and his dad was able to be at peace and not hover over him. It's complicated. You want to see them, but you know you should let go. I know. I went through it with my hubby.

None of it is easy.

I think that you were lucky to have had a close partner and love for all of those years. *A close partnership like that is hard to come by. But, that doesn't make it any easier. I know. Nothing makes it easier when you have a pain in your heart.*

I hope time eases some of this for you. I really do. I hope it helps for you to know that there are people who understand.

FORUM – *During one of my darkest times of my life, I had a dream about my cousin, Tommy, that I was close to. He hugged me and basically said that everything will be all right. The love I felt was so real, and it really helped me out. My cousin, Tommy, was killed in Vietnam.*

His son was born while he was there, and he never got to see him, but the young man looks so much like him.

FORUM – *When my dad died, I found him on the floor. He had a final, fatal heart attack. I was in total shock, and alone. No family around. Keith was in Connecticut, hours away. The firemen/rescue workers took me home, a few doors away. I had to face doing the funeral alone, and calling my sisters and family that lived in other states. I was so overwhelmed with grief that I had passed out. Later that night when I went to bed, I CLEARLY saw my dad's face looking at me and smiling and a huge feeling of peace came over me. I suddenly knew I could handle it and do whatever needed to be done.*

As time went on, every so often I would smell a smell that I knew was my dad. I would be alone in the house, and it was a smell that was was in my 20s. I don't smell that smell as often anymore, but once in a while he is still there.

A couple of my sisters and my half brother told me that they had the same experience with smelling him. So I know it wasn't just me.

I do believe the spirit lingers on and stays with our loved ones. For how long, who knows, but I know it is real.

FORUM – *Many in my faith believe you go straight to Heaven upon death if you are saved. As for me, I believe you either go straight to Heaven or you are in the presence of Heaven and possibly in a dream state until the judgment day. We also believe that we will all know each other in heaven, but I don't see any evidence that a marriage on earth will continue in Heaven because it won't need to be, as we will have perfect lives and there will be no voids to fill.*

God is faithful to save sinners.

The good news is you can know for sure that you are saved. The Bible (King James Version) is THE WORD OF GOD. You must believe with the Bible says about Jesus and salvation. Many different things are taught in the world today about God – about Jesus – Heaven – Hell – Sin and men and women. But only the Word of God can be relied on. God is Faithful and he has preserved his word and protected it from all error.

To be saved, you must believe THE WORD OF GOD. The bible says all have sinned, and come short of the glory of God. Romans 3:23 -- The Bible says there is not righteous, no not one, Rom. 3:10. This is why Jesus Christ died on the cross, was buried, and rose again the third day. Because all are sinners and condemned to eternal punishment in hell and not capable of doing good enough to go to Heaven. Romans 5:8 – But God commendeth his love toward us, in that we were sinners, Christ died for us. God's love (grace) saves all who believe that Jesus is the SON OF GOD. Romans 10:9-10 – That if thou shalt confess with thy mouth the Lord Jesus and shalt BELIEVE IN THINE HEART that GOD hath RAISED him from the dead, THOU SHALT BE SAVED – For with the HEART man Believeth unto righteousness; and with the mouth confession is made unto salvation.

You turn to God from sin and unbelief, and God will save you from sin, and give you everlasting life. He will make you a new creature with new desires and sin will not rule over you anymore. Read John 5:24, John 10:28, Eph. 2:8-9-10, Isaiah 32:17.

FORUM *– Some people believe we won't know each other in Heaven, because we would be sad if someone we love did not make it. Jesus said he goes to prepare a place for us. Also, Jesus told the thief on the cross that he would be with him in paradise. So I guess God's children when they die, they go and spend their time with Jesus waiting for the Judgment Day. All we can do is remember the good times we had and enjoy what time we have left with the love once we have left on earth with us now. My grandmother and I were very close. She died 10 years ago, and I still cry sometimes when I think about her.*

AND NOW FOR A LITTLE HUMOR TO BREAK UP THE GRIEF - FROM THE FORUM … COUNTRY FUNERAL STORY

As a young minister in Kentucky, I was asked by a funeral director to hold a grave-side service for a homeless man, who had no family or friends. The funeral was to be held in a new cemetery way back in the country, and this man would be the first to be buried there.

I was not familiar with the backwoods area, and I soon became lost.

Being a typical man, I did not stop to ask for directions. I finally arrived an hour late.

I saw the backhoe and the open grave, but the hearse was nowhere in sight. The digging crew was eating lunch. I apologized to the workers for my tardiness, and I stepped to the side of the open grave. There, I saw the vault lid already in place. I assured the workers I would not hold them up for long, as I told them that this was the proper thing to do.

The workers gathered around the grave and stood silently, as I began to pour out my heart and soul. As I preached about "looking forward to a brighter tomorrow" and "the glory that is to come," the workers began to say "Amen," "Praise the Lord," and "Glory!" The fervor of these men truly inspired me. So, I preached and I preached like I had never preached like I had never preached before, all the way from Genesis to Revelations.

I finally closed the lengthy service with a prayer, thanked the men, and walked to my car. As I was opening the door and taking off my coat, I heard one of the workers say to another, "I ain't NEVER seen nothin' like that before, and I've been puttin' in septic tanks for thirty years."

ANOTHER STORY – LIFE AFTER DEATH

"Do you believe in life after death?" the boss asked one of his employees.

"Yes, sir," the new employee replied.

"Well, then that makes everything just fine," the boss went on. "After you left early yesterday to go to your grandmother's funeral, she stopped in to see you!

PALM SUNDAY

It was Palm Sunday, and because of a sore throat, five-year-old Johnny stayed home from church with a sitter. When the family returned home, they were carrying several palm branches. The boy asked what they were for. "People held them over Jesus' head as he walked by."

"Wouldn't you know it," the boy fumed, "The one Sunday I don't go, he shows up!"

CHILDREN'S SERMON

One Easter Sunday morning as the minister was preaching the children's sermon, he reached into his bag of props, and pulled out an egg. He pointed at the egg and asked the children, "What's in here?"

"I know!" a little boy exclaimed. "Pantyhose!!"

SUPPORT A FAMILY

The prospective father-in-law asked, "Young man, can you support a family?"

The surprised groom-to-be replied, "Well no, I was just planning to support your daughter. The rest of you will have to fend for yourselves."

A FINAL WORD FROM BOB ABOUT THE FORUM

To sum it all up, it seems that we, in this life here on earth, are much more prepared to seek answers and to ask questions than we are about being prepared for life after death about our future as spirits in a world made up of spirits. Just as we are not prepared for life at birth, we are not prepared for death. We enter into an unknown world with faith and uncertainty. Our apprehension of what lies ahead depends on our religious faith. It appears that some enter this relationship with God and feel their future is safe in His hands with a promise of eternal life. So without compelling evidence, it seems as though mankind must lean on God's words and pray for Him to accept us into heaven. The key to heaven is through God, so it is important that we prepare ourselves for our judgment. I pray for my wife, Virginia, each night and day.

There are times when the question comes up, "Do you want to have an afterlife?" It would be hard for anyone to assume that a person would choose to refrain from a chance to live on. But have you ever wondered what it would be like? Everlasting life? I have always heard about the wonderful place that God made for those of us who are accepted into heaven. It sounds great. Are there any television, ball games, sports, or loved ones there?

Another question comes up. Do we remember our lives here on earth or are we reprogrammed? Some say yes; others say no. When we are born, we gain a soul, and we share that soul with our bodies. At death we part with our bodies and carry on as spirits. All of our knowledge that we have gain throughout life is gone at death – true or false? Why don't we know the answers to these questions? Are we not supposed to know? Life, death, infinity?

Although our spiritual and religious worlds tell us that there is life after death, we can only hope and pray that God will make us happy.

When you truly examine the world we now live in, it is without a doubt a beautiful place. After seeing this, we can only surmise the place he has prepared for us, but at our death is the day we find out. The topic of reincarnation is often mentioned, but the thought of returning to earth as another form of life does not interest me at all. Just as many of us hope and pray for being reunited with our loved ones is our number one prayer. Without them, there is no everlasting life.

We are all searching for answers and some people seem to think our earth was populated by aliens from another planet and are monitoring our lives. It may be far-fetched, but some seem to accept this idea. Although this concept of life beginning on earth is interesting, it is compatible with or acceptable to most of our religious beliefs. Why is it that many are so sure about their fate at death, when others struggle to understand why we are here, and where we will end up.

In the case before my wife's, Virginia's death, I was confident that life after existed, and many times assured her of this fact. I pointed to all the things here on earth that only God could have created. They all fit together like a giant jigsaw puzzle. But after my wife's death, I began to worry about her. I pray to God each night and day for Him to watch over and protect her. After sixty years together, this love story did not end with her death.

I love you, Dinny. God bless you!

A Note from the Editor ...

The following information, regarding man's various human societies, mythologies, and religions, comes from my high school sociology lecture notes on societies and comparative religion. My voice is that of a high school teacher trying to impart general information to her students regarding these rather controversial topics. My sources are varied, coming from sociology and comparative religion texts, and authors such as John Macionis, Desmond Morris, and *The Complete Idiot's Guide to World Religions,* which was a font of information, as well as various religious sources on the Internet.

The content found herein is meant for general knowledge, and is by no means intended to be interpreted as the authority on the subject of afterlife.

THE STORY OF THE AFTERLIFE

Throughout the evolution of societies, humankind puzzled over death and what happens to the body and soul after we cease to be. The first society is that of the hunter-gatherers, who were nomadic and travelled to their food sources – animals. When the animals were consumed and were gone, these peoples moved to another location where they could find animals for their sustenance. It was an "eat or be eaten" world. There are very few of these societies in existence today, but they can be found in the far reaches of South America, Africa, and Asia.

The next group to evolve naturally was the pastoral society, which began to tame and to herd the animals to be used as food. Once again, these people had to move around because the grasses and plants on which the animals fed disappeared, either because of weather, scarcity, or consumption.

Humans, ever resourceful, eventually began to notice that many of those necessary plants bore fruit and/or seeds which were cultivated and eaten, either by the people or their animals, thus beginning the horticultural society. They were now able to plant and to harvest food for themselves and for their animals. It was at this time that man began to feel safe and to set down roots, thereby developing the earliest civilization, and requiring the assignment of roles. The most important role in this society was the shaman (priest or magic man), who answered questions about life, death, body, and soul, as well as to "cure" illnesses. Men hunted, fished, or tended the domesticated animals, while women and children planted seeds and cared for their "gardens." Since there were now divisions of labor, humankind finally had time to ponder if there was life after death and to develop leisure activities.

The ensuing agricultural, industrial, and post-industrial societies continued to rise, to fall, and to question man's destiny after death. If we look at some of the early civilized mythologies, such as Egyptian, Greek, and Roman, we can see the emergence of religion from these early religious systems.

During the more than three thousand years of ancient Egypt's history, beliefs in the afterlife were recorded. All of these people believed in the afterlife and spent their entire lives preparing for it. In order to be accepted into the afterlife, a person's identity needed to be preserved so that the body had to be intact and to receive sustenance regularly for that body. The final step was judgment in the Hall of Maat (god of Justice), by Horus, god of the sky, and Thoth, recorder of the dead, by comparing the conscience and a feather in a ritual known as the Weighing of the Heart. Heavy hearts were swallowed by a creature with a crocodile head – Devourer of Souls. Good people went to the Happy Fields, where they met Osiris, god of the Underworld. Spells and rituals were created to get a favorable judgment and written in the *Book of the Dead*.

Ancient Greeks feared death because it led to a land called Hades, ruled by the god of the underworld, known also by the same name. After death, a Greek crossed the river, Styx, by being buried with a coin for the boatman, Charon. Then Cerberus, the three-headed guard dog had to be appeased with honey cake. The underworld offered punishment for the bad and pleasure for the good. The Elysian Fields was home for those who were good, and there, it was always sunny and pleasant. Bad ancient Greeks were condemned to torture or went on to be shadows or shades of their previous selves.

Ancient Roman mythology described these believers who viewed the short period of life as a sentence to be served by the spirit before it could be freed to take its place in the Milky Way. If we look at star formations on a clear night, we see Orion, Ursa Major (Big Dipper), Ursa Minor (Little Dipper) and Pegasus (The Winged Horse). To these ancients, life was the spirit's death. It was wrong for a man to commit suicide, because life's purpose was to do good for his world. Those ancient Romans, who spent their lives committed to service and good deeds, observing justice, piety, and honor for family and country, believed they were to spend eternity in the skies and to experience joy forever. Like the ancient Greeks, the Roman underworld, ruled by Pluto, was a place for murderers, thieves, and those who were evil. There are distinct parallels in these mythologies, but now we turn to the major organized world religions, which are discussed here from the oldest to the newest, in order to muse over their doctrines regarding the afterlife.

Hinduism, thought to have begun in 2,000 B.C.E. (Before the Common Era, often coinciding with the birth of Christ), is possibly the most diverse of these religions in that some Hindus are monotheistic (believer in one god) and some are polytheistic (believer in many gods). Some resources state that there are from 300,000 to over 3 million deities in this particular religion. They do agree that life is a series of reincarnations – birth, then death, and rebirth into a higher or lower caste or social level, depending on whether the former life was based on good or evil deeds. It is generally accepted that Nirvana is the aim of all Hindus, for it breaks the cycle of the reincarnations and allows the believer to experience a complete union with the universal creative force. A Hindu's afterlife relies on his/her state of mind at the moment of death. If one passes away at a time of anger, violence, or hopelessness, then he or she enters a dark world filled with those who die similarly. This religion also embraces the doctrine of Karma in which the believer is held to be accountable for every thought, word, or deed during his or her life time. These followers believe that there are two ways to achieve the state of enlightenment either through good works to family and community or through knowledge.

The next religion, Judaism, circa 1,500 – 1,350 B.C.E., posits several theories regarding the afterlife. One such believes that death will eventually lead to resurrection in a future world. Another sees afterlife as a shadowy placed called *Sheol*, filled with darkness and silence, located in low places. It is God who puts souls there. A third interpretation is that Eden is the eternal destination for the righteous, and it is described as a place of great joy and peace. A fourth theory of the afterlife for the wicked has its foundation in a dark pit, and those who are there are punished for a time and then are either annihilated or continue to be punished for all eternity. Jews believe that it is important to lead a Godly life by education, religious piety, and completion of good deeds without personal benefit.

While Buddhism comes from Hinduism, it was established some 1,500 years later in 563 B.C.E., by Siddhartha Gautama. Like Hinduism, it embraces reincarnation, karma, and Nirvana. These believers emphasize that the destination of the soul after death depends on one's karma, and that if one's human life was filled with anger, desire, and ignorance, the soul will not get to a destination closer to enlightenment. There are many realms into which one's soul may be reborn – human, animal, "jealous gods," and/or "the heavens." These believers posit that there is a heaven – Nirvana, beyond comprehension, and a hell, which is not permanent, for it is a period of punishment, then purification.

On the other hand, Japanese Buddhists have very specific times and stages of the afterlife, for they believe that forty-nine days after death, the spirit is separated into three stages. The first occurs from between a half day to four days – a time when the spirit becomes aware that it has left its body and sees the light; the strength of which depends on how spiritually developed the spirit has become. The second stage is where the spirit meets both peaceful and violent deities in hallucinogenic sets. The final stage is dependent on whether or not the spirit survives these encounters; if there are no problems, the spirit reaches Nirvana (ultimate heaven). If the spirit does not survive, it returns to earth for rebirth. Spiritual purity decides whether a person's spirit moves up or down in status during reincarnation.

At about 551 before the Common Era, Confucianism was begun. There are some who believe that it is more than a religion, perhaps even a philosophy. The main proponent of this religion, Confucius, thought that life and death are determined by fate, wealth, and nobility, which are delineated by heaven, emphasizing life, rather than death. During life, one should meet one's responsibility in realizing the ideal of a harmonious society through several relationships: parenthood, government, spouses, siblings and friends. Man should consider it his duty to know the workings of the way to heaven. Confucius neglected the world after death and believed that man can be immortal by setting a good example in virtue, achieving a great career, or leaving behind great writings.

We all know that Christianity began with the birth of Christ and that His birth heralded the Common Era, which is dated at 1 and evolved into a religious movement throughout His short lifetime to 33 C.E. because of his teachings. The foundation of this religion generally lies in believing that death is a passage from earthly life to the new, everlasting life, as promised by The Messiah. Belief in God and Jesus Christ as well as a life based on faith, hope, and charity determine whether that eternal life is spent in heaven where the soul experiences unbelievable happiness and infinity with God. Those who have eschewed God, and lead a sinful life, go to hell where those souls encounter nothing but pain punishment for eternity. Catholics, on the other hand, believe in an additional alternative – purgatory where those who are not quite purified go to receive spiritual cleansing, once done, eventually leading to heaven. We also know that the diverse Christian denominations preach their own variations of life after death, and are too numerous to mention here.

Shintoism, is believed to have begun as a formal religion in 500 C.E in Japan. Before that time, it was a form of nature worship. This belief emphasizes cleanliness, harmony and beauty in life. There is no omnipotent god found in this religion, only divine spirits, and it can be practiced along with Buddhism. Shintoism does not want people to focus on death, for if one fears it, he or she will not get the most out of life – "the here and the now." These worshippers believe that the dead body is very powerful and impure; therefore, it is a crime to harm one.

Finally, the newest world religion is Islam, begun by Mohammed in 570 C.E. Muslims, both Sunni and Shiite, believe that after death, a soul remains in its grave until Judgment Day or the Day of Reckoning, at which time Allah recreates the soul's physical body. God judges the resurrected body according to its deeds. Paradise is for the righteous and those who submit to Allah's will. It is a place filled with spiritual and physical pleasure forever. Muslim warriors who die in battle for Allah's cause go directly to paradise. Hell is where evil doers spend eternity experiencing spiritual and physical torture, and Muslims believe that Islam's enemies go directly to hell when they die.

In summary, after death, most world religions agree that those who lead good lives and have faith in a particular deity go to heaven, where there is no pain, just eternal pleasure, whatever that is, and which is probably specific to the believer. Conversely, those who commit evil deeds or who do not fulfill the tenets set down by that particular religion go to hell, where they experience eternal punishment. We can also see that there is a specific human need to believe that at the death of the physical body there is an afterlife for the soul, which evolved during man's early societies when there was time away from danger and work to ponder such wonderments.

EPILOGUE

Not very many men have the opportunity to share a life with a woman who wanted nothing more than to make me happy. She was content with her life and loved her kids and her home. Woe is the person who picked on Dinny's kids. Our home is close to a hundred years old, yet she loved it like a castle. She tackled any job from laying tile to painting the rooms. Her yard was her treasure chest with a lot of knick-knacks of all kinds with a lot of angels decorating it, because she had a strong attraction to angels. One year she had me build two wooden deer for the backyard – a buck and a doe. She was so proud of them that each year, she cleaned and painted them. Her life seemed to be aimed at making other people happy. Many times when we went shopping, she came home with things for the kids or for me, and when I asked her to buy something for herself, she shrugged it off and said, "Next payday." Our daughter, Carol, and she made it a ritual to start buying presents for the grand kids on the first of January of each year. By the time Christmas came, there was a gigantic pile of clothes and toys for the kids.

Many times, years ago, when she was sick and in the hospital, I sneaked down to a woman's store and asked a girl whom I knew there to pick out sexy lingerie. When she came home from the hospital, I had those things hanging around the house with signs that read, "Welcome Home, Dinny," and "I Love You, Honey." When we went on vacation to Florida, she never went into the pool because she was very upset if her hair became wet, and as she grew older, she refused to put on a bathing suit, even though she had a great figure. She always knew that I liked long hair, and she went out of her way to take care of that beautiful blond hair. Every night in her later years, she got out her curlers and rolled them up in her hair. Even later in life, I told her, "Do not worry about me, get your hair cut so that you don't have to take so much time

93

with it." To her very end, she looked beautiful. When she went shopping with our daughter, Carol often became upset with her because Dinny always said, "Carol, I have to get home. Your dad will be mad at me." I never once said anything to her about how long she stayed, but she was like me, she missed me just as I missed her. We were inseparable and very happy just being together at home watching television, or going out to a restaurant.

It is very hard for me to even write this because the memories are etched in my brain, and my heart aches for her. To every couple who has this kind of loving relationship with a spouse, life is a blink of an eye. Make every minute count together. We were always laying money away for a rainy day and not doing more things together to enjoy life. As I look back now, I feel so sad that I did not insist that we spend it and let it rain.

Virginia was loved by all who met her. As a business partner, she spent hours upon hours helping with our commercial fishing and charter businesses.

Years ago, she strung nets from our kitchen to the front room, surprising me when I came home from the power house working three to eleven shift. She made up a two hundred ten foot net, string ties that are six inches apart on top and bottom lines. She often met me at the door with coffee and a sandwich, or a martini and a nightgown. I swear, when a person is young, he or she is bound by sex and adventure, but as one ages, one begins to realize how much a loved one means to him or her. That is when we really find out what love is all about. It's not just kissing and hugging, but sharing a life together. The smell of her hair, the feel of her in one's arms, and the enjoyment felt from doing something that she likes – that's love.

Virginia spent a lifetime making me into a man, but she did it with love and affection. Her heart has been transplanted into mine. I will never ever lose that love that I have for her. This house that we shared for sixty years is now empty. She was the one who made it a home. It is way too big for me now, but I cannot bring myself to sell it, because the memories are just too strong yet. I feel the same about her car; I don't need two cars, but I just can't sell it.

Above everything else, Virginia loved her kids as she loved me. I recall that when our son, Bob left for Vietnam, she was very heartbroken. When we had the chance to meet him in Hawaii on his R & R, we mortgaged our home again and flew out to see him. It was a five-hour flight to Los Angeles, and another long flight to Hawaii. On that leg of the trip, a flight attendant spilled a big cup of coffee on Virginia's blouse. She gave her a big towel to cover up, and had her take her top off to wash it. The pilot came back and apologized to her. I do not go through one minute of my life now without thinking of the wonderful life we had together. I thank God for the years of happiness that I enjoyed with this wonderful woman. I pray to God that she is free of pain and happy now with her deceased family.

My Final Thoughts

Today is Wednesday June 16th 2010 my book is finished and it is now in the hands of the publisher, As I look back at my life with Virginia I can only Pray we will be together again some day, I have had a fantastic life survived WW-2, came home to Marry a beautiful gal named Virginia Traxler she made my life complete,

I dedicated this book to her because she was a Angel sent down from heaven, As I look back at our life together I can only remember the great times we had together, for 60 years.

She Impressed me with her devotion to our kids and family, she never once complained, The secret to our marriage was we enjoyed each other, and we spent as much time as we could together, Virginia was in pain most of our later life together but she kept up her spirits and always had a smile on her face .Today on my boat out in the lake I found a penny laying on the deck,,! She still lets me know she is with me yet!!

Capt R A Jaycox